The Battle
of North Cape

Campaign Chronicles

The Battle of North Cape

The Death Ride of the *Scharnhorst*, 1943

Angus Konstam

Campaign Chronicles
Series Editor

Christopher Summerville

Pen & Sword
MARITIME

First published in Great Britain in 2009
Reprinted in this format in 2011& 2013 by
PEN & SWORD MARITIME
An imprint of
Pen & Sword Books Ltd
47 Church Street
Barnsley,
South Yorkshire
S70 2AS

ISBN 978-1-84884-557-2

A CIP catalogue record for this book
is available from the British Library

Typeset in Sabon 11/13.5pt by
Concept, Huddersfield

Printed and bound by CPI Group (UK) Ltd, Croydon, CR0 4YY

Pen & Sword Books Ltd incorporates the Imprints of Pen & Sword Aviation,
Pen & Sword Family History, Pen & Sword Maritime, Pen & Sword Military,
Pen & Sword Discovery, Pen & Sword Politics, Pen & Sword Archaeology,
Pen & Sword Atlas, Wharncliffe Local History, Wharncliffe True Crime,
Wharncliffe Transport, Pen & Sword Select, Pen & Sword Military Classics,
Leo Cooper, The Praetorian Press, Claymore Press, Remember When,
Seaforth Publishing and Frontline Publishing

For a complete list of Pen & Sword titles please contact
PEN & SWORD BOOKS LIMITED
47 Church Street, Barnsley, South Yorkshire, S70 2AS, England
E-mail: enquiries@pen-and-sword.co.uk
Website: www.pen-and-sword.co.uk

Contents

Maps and Illustrations

Maps

Maps and Illustrations

The *Scharnhorst*, pictured from the deck of her sister ship the *Gneisenau*

The *Tirpitz*, anchored in the Altenfjord

Survivors of the *Scharnhorst* (1)

Generaladmiral Otto Schniewind

Survivors of the *Scharnhorst* (2)

The German yacht *Grille* ('Cricket')

A convoy gathered in Loch Ewe

German 'Narvik' class destroyer *Z-33*

The quarterdeck of the *Scharnhorst*

The *Scharnhorst* in heavy seas

Rear Admiral Robert Burnett

Admiral Bruce Fraser

Commander Ralph Fisher

Konter-Admiral Erich Bey

Kapitän-zur-See Fritz Hintze

Grossadmiral Karl Dönitz

The *Tirpitz*, the *Admiral Scheer* and the *Admiral Hipper* on exercise in Norwegian waters

HMS *Belfast*, the flagship of Rear Admiral Burnett

HMS *Sheffield*

HMS *Jamaica*

The heavy cruiser HMS *Norfolk*

Two small 'Flower' class corvettes

'Tribal' class destroyers such as HMS *Ashanti* were powerful, fast and well-armed

HMS *Duke of York*, photographed during her triumphant return to Scapa Flow on New Year's Day, 1944

A German sailor, calling out to be rescued from the sea

Admiral Fraser and his captains, photographed on the deck of HMS *Duke of York* in Scapa Flow in early 1944

Maps

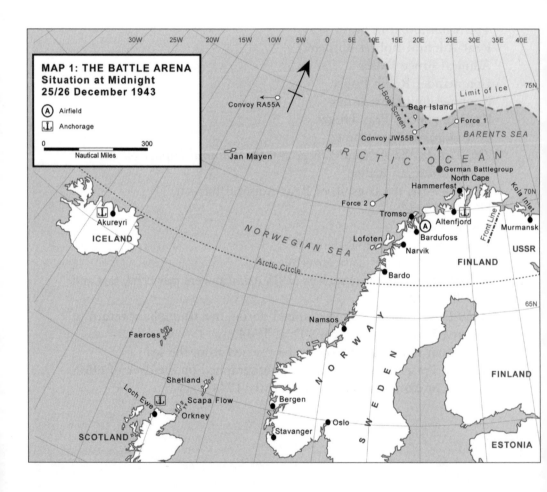

MAP 1: THE BATTLE ARENA
Situation at Midnight
25/26 December 1943

(A) Airfield

[L] Anchorage

0 _____ 300
Nautical Miles

Convoy RA55A

Limit of Ice

75N

U-Boat Screen

Bear Island

Force 1

Convoy JW55B

BARENTS SEA

Jan Mayen

A R C T I C   O C E A N

German Battlegroup
North Cape

Hammerfest

Kola Inlet

70N

Force 2

Tromso

Altenfjord

Murmansk

Akureyri

Bardufoss

Lofoten

ICELAND

N O R W E G I A N   S E A

Narvik

USSR

Front Line

FINLAND

Arctic Circle

Bardo

65N

Namsos

Faeroes

N
O
R
W
A
Y

S
W
E
D
E
N

FINLAND

Shetland

Loch Ewe

[L] Scapa Flow

Bergen

Orkney

Oslo

SCOTLAND

Stavanger

ESTONIA

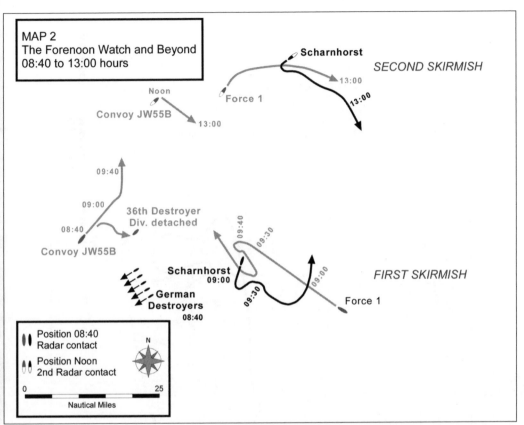

MAP 2
The Forenoon Watch and Beyond
08:40 to 13:00 hours

SECOND SKIRMISH

Scharnhorst
13:00
13:00

Noon
Convoy JW55B
13:00
Force 1

09:40
09:00
08:40
Convoy JW55B

36th Destroyer
Div. detached

09:40
09:30

Scharnhorst
09:00

German
Destroyers
08:40

09:30
09:00

Force 1

FIRST SKIRMISH

Position 08:40
Radar contact

Position Noon
2nd Radar contact

N

0   25
Nautical Miles

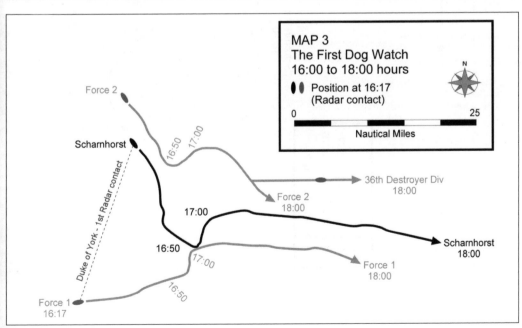

MAP 3
The First Dog Watch
16:00 to 18:00 hours

N

Position at 16:17
(Radar contact)

0   25
Nautical Miles

Force 2

Scharnhorst

16:50
17:00

Duke of York - 1st Radar contact

36th Destroyer Div
18:00

17:00

Force 2
18:00

16:50

17:00

Scharnhorst
18:00

Force 1
18:00

Force 1
16:17

16:50

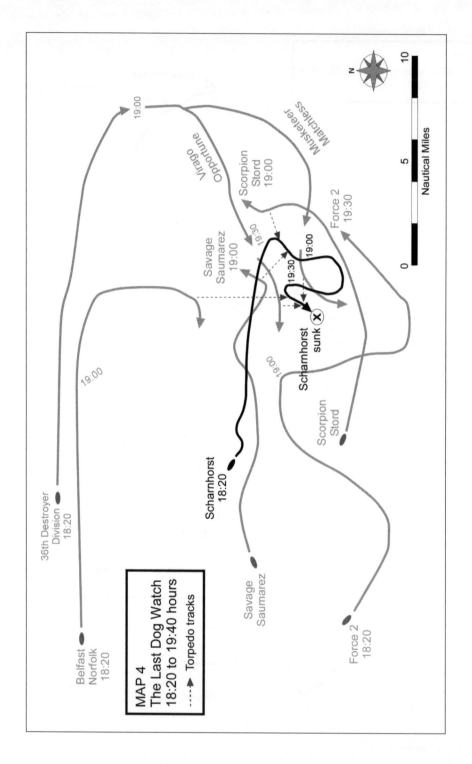

MAP 4
The Last Dog Watch
18:20 to 19:40 hours

----▶ Torpedo tracks

Nautical Miles

0   5   10

36th Destroyer
Division
18:20

Belfast
Norfolk
18:20

19:00

19:00

Viragus
Opportune

Scorpion
Stord
19:00

Musketeer
Matchless

Force 2
19:30

Savage
Saumarez
19:00

19:30

19:30

19:00

19:00

Scharnhorst
sunk ⊗

Scorpion
Stord

Scharnhorst
18:20

Savage
Saumarez

Force 2
18:20

Background

This naval battle, fought to a grim conclusion amid dark and stormy water off the northern tip of Norway, was a struggle that has all but been forgotten. It was the climax of a long and hard-fought naval campaign, which for various reasons, has been largely bypassed by historians in their eagerness to recount more dramatic tales of warfare. However, the Battle of North Cape was an engagement that deserves to be placed among the truly decisive naval encounters of the Second World War. In its way it was every bit as important as the great carrier battles fought out in the Pacific, and probably of greater strategic significance than the sinking of the *Bismark* or the *Graf Spee*. This book is a humble attempt to raise awareness of the events that led to the sinking of Germany's last operational capital warship, and to honour the men of both sides who fought and died in those bleak, freezing waters almost two-thirds of a century ago.

Introduction
The Battle of North Cape was a naval struggle the like of which was never seen again. While the commanders of both sides embraced, or at least made use of, the new technologies of naval warfare – aircraft, submarines, radar and electronic surveillance – this was still a battle fought in the old style: a duel to the death using guns and torpedoes, fired or launched by surface warships. It was the last naval battle fought using these tools of surface combat alone, a clash of battleships, those long-departed gun-armed titans of the seas. In fact, the Battle of North Cape was a naval clash that invokes many superlatives. It was the last naval engagement in history involving a major unit of the German Kriegsmarine. It was one of the first where

The Battle of North Cape

search radar and radar fire control played a major part in the outcome. Above all, it was a strategic victory that ensured the continued supply of the Soviet war effort. That winter the Red Army was preparing for a new offensive, which, in the following year, would take it to the borders of Hitler's Germany. Each convoy carried the equivalent of an armoured corps, and every ship that made it safely to Murmansk would help tip the balance in favour of the Allied cause.

One other important factor set the battle apart. It was highly unusual to fight a major naval engagement in the Arctic twilight, or during the darkness that falls within two hours of noon. This spectacular naval clash was fought to a conclusion in the pitch dark, or at least in a dim twilight, and in seas so mountainous that the small destroyers were in as much danger of succumbing to the elements as they were to German shells. Then there was the cold – the freezing, all-pervading icy cold, which tested the endurance of sailors of both sides as they manned their deck guns or lookout positions. Worse still, this was a fight to the death, the inevitable consequence being that those sailors who managed to escape from their burning, sinking ship were pitched into the freezing waters of the Barents Sea. For them, their chances of survival were slim.

Those sailors of both sides who survived the battle have tried to recount their experiences as best they could, and many of these accounts have been woven into the narrative of this book. Mere words could hardly express the sheer desperate horror of watching your shipmates maimed beside you, or drifting in the freezing oil-covered water with little hope of rescue, and with consciousness slipping away. This book can only capture a fragment of what these young men experienced. And the word 'young' is an important one. The average age of the men who survived the sinking of the *Scharnhorst* was just twenty-one. Many of the crews of the British, Canadian and Polish warships that took part in the battle were equally youthful, although many had already experienced the harsh realities of naval warfare. For the most part they were commanded by junior officers and senior ratings little older themselves, although on both sides the more senior officers and ratings were battle-hardened men of experience, capable of imbuing their young subordinates with the professionalism for which the navies of both sides were renowned.

Background

Then there were the admirals – the men whose decisions set events in motion that would lead to this clash of titans, and on whose shoulders rested the responsibility for so many lives. Admiral Bruce Fraser and Konter-Admiral Heinrich Bey were the men who fought what was ultimately a very personal naval duel, albeit one involving ships, aircraft and submarines rather than pistols or swords. These two men were very different, but each carried with him the weight of naval tradition, and the aspirations and objectives of their Service. Of the two, Bey was the most hamstrung. While he maintained full operational control over his Battlegroup, he was still expected to follow the orders of his superiors – Generaladmiral Schniewind in Kiel, and Grossadmiral Dönitz in Berlin. While he enjoyed the theoretical support of the Kriegsmarine's U-boat arm and of the Luftwaffe stationed in Norway, cumbersome chains of command and inter-service rivalry meant that, for the most part, he could rely on little assistance. By contrast, Fraser enjoyed complete strategic control over his forces, and while he was ultimately answerable to the British Admiralty, he was given a free hand in waging the naval battle his own way. Ultimately, the faith of the Admiralty in Fraser's abilities would be fully justified.

The Battle of North Cape was almost the last chapter of a long naval campaign. Since the summer of 1941 the great logistical operation of the Arctic convoys had tested the resolve of the British Navy and merchant marine, and placed an immense strain on Britain's meagre resources. When the United States entered the war in December 1941 the operation took on a fresh momentum, and for the best part of the next two years it remained a vital lifeline that helped keep the Soviet Union in the war. Of course, these convoys were as much a political necessity as a military one, demonstrating a solidarity between the Western Allies and the Soviet Union that was geographically impossible on the battlefield. For their part, the Germans were equally aware of the political symbolism, which for them made the disruption of these convoys even more important.

Hitler invaded the Soviet Union in late June 1941, and within weeks it had become clear that the Red Army was losing the campaign. By August more than half a million Soviet soldiers had been captured, and German columns were driving deep into the heart of Russia. While the Red Army hurriedly did what it could to prevent the capture

The Battle of North Cape

of Moscow and Leningrad, Soviet industrial plants were shipped east of the Ural Mountains, beyond the reach of the invaders. It would take time for these factories to be reassembled, and for the production lines to begin producing the tanks, planes and guns the Red Army so desperately needed in its fight for survival. To help ease the pressure, Churchill offered to send whatever aid he could, and so, in August 1941, the first 'Arctic convoy' of seven merchant ships arrived in Murmansk. Eight more convoys would follow before the end of the year. All made it through safely, with the loss of just one merchant ship, sunk by a U-boat.

However, the Germans were now aware of the importance of these convoys, and diverted air and naval resources to deal with them. The core of the German naval presence in Norwegian waters was the battleship *Tirpitz*, supported by a flotilla of destroyers. She was soon joined by the pocket battleships *Admiral Scheer* and *Lützow*, and the heavy cruiser *Admiral Hipper*. U-boats were moved north, as were whole squadrons of Luftwaffe bombers and long-range reconnaissance planes. Until then, the biggest threat to the seamen of the Arctic convoys was the weather. After all, they were sailing through some of the least hospitable waters in the world. Between January and June 1942 the Germans gradually increased the pressure on the convoys. There were nine outward bound and seven homeward bound convoys during this period, and losses increased almost every time. By June the Allies had lost twenty-one merchant ships, three light cruisers and two destroyers in the battles to force these convoys through, while German casualties were limited to just two destroyers. It was now mid-summer – a time of near constant light in Arctic waters. The Admiralty requested that the convoys be suspended until winter, but for political reasons Churchill ordered them to continue.

The result was the disaster of Convoy PQ 17. In late June 1942 this convoy of thirty-six merchant ships sailed from Iceland, bound for Murmansk's Kola Inlet. Threat of a sortie by German surface warships led to the decision that the convoy should scatter. Even more bizarrely, the heavy escorts – including the battleships HMS *Duke of York* and USS *Washington* – were withdrawn. Only eleven of the merchantmen made it safely into port. Two were forced to return to Iceland, and twenty-three were sunk by German aircraft and U-boats. It was a tough lesson in convoy management and strategy, bought at the expense of hundreds of lives. Convoys were suspended, and by the time they were renewed in September, the British and their Allies had worked hard to learn from their mistakes. Between September and December one outward bound and two homeward bound convoys successfully ran the German gauntlet, and although sixteen merchant ships and a minesweeper were lost, the convoy escorts accounted for over forty German aircraft and four U-boats. It was clear that the Germans would no longer enjoy air and naval superiority in the Barents Sea.

Consequently, in December, the decision was made to launch a naval sortie against the next convoy, JW 51A. The result was a confused engagement known as the Battle of the Barents Sea, where Rear Admiral Burnett's British cruisers successfully kept the German pocket battleship *Lützow* and heavy cruiser *Admiral Scheer* from reaching the convoy. As a result the convoy made it to Murmansk without loss. The most significant result of this inconclusive battle was that Hitler lost his patience with the Kriegsmarine and its expensive capital ships. When he learned that they had been driven off by British light cruisers he flew into a rage, and ordered the dismantling of the surface fleet. Grossadmiral Raeder resigned in protest, and was replaced by Karl Dönitz, the architect of the German U-boat fleet.

The British suspended convoy operations in March, and planned to renew them in November, when the near-constant Arctic darkness hid them from German aircraft. For their part, the Germans used the time to prepare for the renewal of the battle. Dönitz persuaded Hitler to spare the large capital ships of the Kriegsmarine, and he even managed to reinforce the Northern Battlegroup – the collection of powerful warships stationed in the Altenfjord, near the northernmost tip of Norway. In March 1943 the battlecruiser *Scharnhorst* was ordered to join the Battlegroup, an addition that greatly increased the latent threat these German warships posed to the convoys.

The *Scharnhorst* was widely regarded as 'a lucky ship'. She had been mined and torpedoed, but she always managed to avoid the serious damage that seemed to plague her sister ship, the *Gneisenau*. Her motto – *Scharnhorst immer voran!* ('*Scharnhorst* ever onwards') was more than a slogan – for the sailors it testified to a belief that she would always make it home safely, regardless of the odds stacked against her. She was named after a Prussian commander in the wars fought against Napoleon, and she seemed to epitomise the resilience of the Prussian warrior class. Her launch in June 1936 had been witnessed by Hitler, who at the time was as satisfied as his naval commanders that she represented the very latest word in power, strength and armoured protection – naval perfection encased in hardened Krupp steel. But for all her skirmishes off Norway, in the Atlantic or in the English Channel, her fighting abilities had never been fully tested. That great trial lay ahead of her, and would take place in the cold waters off North Cape.

The Rivals

The two admirals who squared off against each other near North Cape that December could hardly have been more different, nor could the forces at their disposal. One was a former destroyer commander, who seemed to have little grasp of strategy, and whose preparation for the operation left much to be desired. The other was a consummate professional, a gunnery specialist whose long and distinguished naval career seemed to have been a preparation for the challenge that faced him during the battle. One commanded a formidable fighting warship, whose combination of armour and speed made her all but unstoppable. The other commanded a polyglot force of cruisers, destroyers and a battleship – a force that relied on radar, aggression and firepower to secure victory over its opponent.

Konter-Admiral Erich 'Achmed' Bey (1898–1943) was not the Kriegsmarine's first choice as the commander of its Northern Battle-group, but chance and circumstance placed him on the admiral's bridge of the *Scharnhorst* when she sailed from the Altenfjord. He joined the Imperial German Navy in 1916, in the immediate after-math of the Battle of Jutland, and he served in destroyers until the war ended two years later. He remained in the Reichsmarine during the Weimar years, and the Kriegsmarine during the rise of Hitler. By 1940 he was a Fregattenkapitän (Commander), and commanded the 4th Destroyer Flotilla during the German invasion of Norway. On 10 April that year he distinguished himself by leading a naval counter-attack during the First Battle of Narvik, which resulted in the sinking of two British destroyers. This achievement was nullified three days later when the British returned, and in the Second Battle of Narvik

Background

that followed, Bey lost his entire command of eight destroyers – the core of the German destroyer fleet.

Despite this he was lauded as a hero, awarded the Knight's Cross, and promoted to Kapitän-zur-See (Captain). He was named *Führer der Zerstörer* (Flag Officer Destroyers), and charged with restoring the morale and efficiency of the Kriegsmarine's battered destroyer fleet. His first real chance came in February 1942 during 'The Channel Dash', when his destroyers helped the *Scharnhorst*, *Gniesenau* and *Prinz Eugen* run the gauntlet of British air and naval forces as it ran through the English Channel – one of the most dramatic and successful chapters in the Kriegsmarine's short history. There is little doubt that Bey was a highly competent destroyer commander. A colleague described him as a man of massive build, an excellent seaman, and a born destroyer commander. However, his problems began when he was promoted due to his achievements, and made a Konter-Admiral (Rear Admiral). As a dashing light force commander he was without peer. As an admiral he was out of his depth.

On being appointed to flag command he supposedly commented that: 'the last time I was aboard a capital ship it was as a cadet.' However, at first he continued to command the Kriegsmarine's destroyers, and his vessels performed well in support of the Northern Battlegroup during 1942 and early 1943. Then, in early November 1943, the Battlegroup commander, Konter-Admiral Kummetz, returned home on sick leave and Grossadmiral Dönitz appointed Erich Bey in his place. Bey now commanded a handful of destroyers, the damaged *Tirpitz*, and the battle-ready *Scharnhorst*. During his seven weeks in command he seemed to show little interest in his ships and men, or in the formulation of plans. Of course he was hampered by a lack of staff – many of Kummetz's experienced officers returned to Germany with the admiral, leaving the Battlegroup short-handed. Bey also had his doubts about the success of any operation – he considered the *Scharnhorst* too vulnerable to risk, and would have preferred to rely on destroyers alone to harass the enemy convoys. He also lacked intelligence about Allied naval strength, and the Luftwaffe was less than cooperative when it came to providing reconnaissance cover of Arctic waters.

In late December the sortie of the *Scharnhorst* – codenamed Operation Ostfront ('East Front') was thrust upon him at short notice.

The Battle of North Cape

His skeleton staff on board the *Tirpitz* had little opportunity to consider tactics, prepare the inexperienced crews of the Battlegroup's warships for action during the Arctic winter, or even to fully brief the commanders involved. Bey was simply told to prepare his force for action and within two days was ordered to lead the Battlegroup forth. In these circumstances it is hard not to feel a little sorry for Erich Bey. With the benefit of hindsight it is all to easy to fault his performance, and certainly Dönitz made him the scapegoat for the failure of Operation Ostfront. Bey needed a combination of good intelligence, surprise and luck to succeed. During the battle that followed, all three would elude him.

The difference between Bey and his British opponent could hardly have been more marked. Admiral Bruce Fraser (1888–1981) joined the Royal Navy in 1902, showing promise from the start. In 1911 he specialised in Naval Gunnery, and when the First World War broke out he was serving as the gunnery officer on the cruiser HMS *Minerva*, before serving in the same capacity for the rest of the war on the new battleship, HMS *Resolution*. In 1920 he was captured by the Red Army during a landing at Baku, on the Caspian Sea, and spent six months as a prisoner-of-war. On his release he returned to Britain and served in a string of increasingly prestigious staff appointments, both afloat and ashore. He was promoted Captain in 1926 and was finally given his own command – the light cruiser, HMS *Effingham*.

In 1933 Fraser became the Director of Naval Ordnance, where one of his tasks was to supervise the design and testing of the Navy's new 14-inch guns, mounted in quadruple turrets. A decade later he would use these same guns in action against the *Scharnhorst*. In 1936 he was given command of the aircraft carrier HMS *Glorious*, making him one of the few senior officers to realise the potential of naval airpower – and its limitations. Four years later the same carrier would be sunk by the *Scharnhorst* off the coast of Norway. For Fraser, the cornering of the *Scharnhorst* therefore involved an element of revenge. He was promoted to the rank of Rear Admiral in January 1938, and served as Chief of Staff to the Commander of the Mediterranean Fleet during the political crisis caused by the Spanish Civil War. On the eve of hostilities he returned to Britain to become the Third Sea Lord, where he was responsible for improving the fighting ability of the Service – a task for which he was admirably suited.

Background

Fraser was promoted to Vice-Admiral in May 1940, and in June 1942 he was named as the Deputy Commander of the Home Fleet. In May 1943 the gifted Admiral Tovey stepped down to take up a new position, and Fraser replaced him as the new Commander of the Home Fleet, based in Scapa Flow. Fraser was given the acting rank of Admiral, a flag rank that was only officially confirmed two months after the Battle of North Cape.

What really set Fraser apart from his contemporaries were his natural skills in leadership. He had the ability to talk with subordinates of any rank and make them feel valued. He genuinely cared for his men and their welfare, and he inspired them. Fraser felt himself privileged to be part of what he regarded as the finest fighting force in the world, and consequently viewed Royal Naval personnel as members of the same elite band, regardless of their experience or status. As a commander he was prone to mixing with his men, and listening to their problems and worries. Despite this, he could be a hard taskmaster, and expected the best from those around him.

Fraser projected a calm, unruffled exterior, and rarely lost his composure, whatever the crisis. He was also highly intelligent, and according to his Flag Lieutenant, Vernon Merry, he spent most afternoons smoking his pipe and thinking. As Merry put it: 'he would fight hypothetical fleet actions, rehearsing dispositions, ranges' – as such he had mentally engaged the *Scharnhorst* dozens of times before he actually brought her to battle. Fraser was a confirmed bachelor, and remained unmarried throughout his life – his first love, after all, was the Service. As an admiral he remains one of the great unsung heroes of the Second World War – a man who did much to influence its course but whose deeds were barely remembered after the guns fell silent.

While Fraser was regarded as a 'thinking admiral', his subordinate, Rear Admiral Robert Burnett (1887–1959), actually made fun of his own intellectual shortcomings. However, he had proven himself as a 'fighting admiral', and was the ideal man to command Fraser's cruiser force. The Scottish-born Burnett entered the Navy in 1902 – the same year as Fraser, and during the First World War had commanded destroyers in the Grand Fleet. He specialised in physical training, and was made a captain in 1930. His commands included the battleship HMS *Rodney*, but he also gained staff experience, and in 1941 was promoted to flag rank. His promotion to Vice-Admiral was announced just days before the *Scharnhorst* operation began. His great skill was that he had a good instinct for naval warfare, although he also inspired great confidence and loyalty from his men. Despite some criticism of Burnett's performance during the Battle of North Cape, Admiral Fraser was well served by his deputy during the fight.

Just as Konter-Admiral Bey and Admiral Fraser were poles apart in terms of experience and professionalism, their two powerful flagships were also very different – the result of two competing schools of naval warfare. The *Scharnhorst* was a battlecruiser, a compromise between the hitting power of a battleship and the speed and range of a cruiser. In the First World War this proved an unhappy combination, but in the case of the *Scharnhorst* and her sister, the *Gneisenau*, the compromise worked well. While the *Scharnhorst*'s 11-inch guns lacked the hitting power of her British counterpart, they could fire faster, and the weight saved allowed for far better armoured protection. In effect, the hull armour of the *Scharnhorst* was proof against the guns of any battleship in the British fleet.

The Germans knew they could never match the British in terms of fleet size. Therefore, they opted for a handful of well-protected ships, whose purpose was not the imposition of global seapower, but the harassment of maritime supply lines. The *Scharnhorst* was therefore designed to cruise independently, or operate in concert with other German warships to interdict enemy convoys – exactly what she was called upon to do in December 1943. For the most part, the Kreigsmarine realised the limitations of their two battlecruisers, and tried to keep them out of harm's way. As we shall see, in December 1943 the Kriegsmarine were forced to risk the *Scharnhorst* in battle, putting into train a sequence of events that would reach a climax when the German battlecruiser encountered her rival flagship, the *Duke of York*.

The *Duke of York* was first and foremost a battleship, built to fight other battleships, either alone or as part of a line of battle. As such she was a floating gunnery platform – everything centred around her main armament of ten 14-inch guns. They fired a 1½-ton shell, and at their maximum elevation of 40° these guns had a range of 36,000 yards (18 nautical miles). Her design was the result of a compromise brought about by the London and Washington Naval Treaties of 1930 and 1936 respectively, which limited the size and armament of new battleships. Her original design called for an armament of nine

Background

15-inch guns in three turrets, but political constraints meant that the Navy was forced to opt for a 14-inch gun instead. But the battleship was well protected, and her main belt was considered adequate protection against the 15-inch shells fired by the latest German or Italian battleships. By 1943 the *Duke of York* was also well provided with radar, and her crew were well versed in firing their guns using both visual and radar guidance. This would prove an inestimable advantage in the battle to come.

Order of Battle

The German Kriegsmarine

Northern Battlegroup Konter-Admiral Bey

KMS *Scharnhorst* ('Scharnhorst' class battlecruiser) Flag of Konter-Admiral Erich Bey

Kap. Fritz Hintze

4th Destroyer Flotilla Kapitän-zur-See Johannesson

Z-29 (1936A 'Narvik' class destroyer)

Flag, Kap. Rolf Johannesson

Korv. Kap. Theodor von Mutius

Z-30 (1936A 'Narvik' class destroyer) Kap. Karl Lampe

Z-33 (1936A (Mob) 'Narvik' class destroyer) Kap. Erich Holtorf

Z-34 (1936A (Mob) 'Narvik' class destroyer) Korv. Kap. Karl Hetz

Z-38 (1936A (Mob) 'Narvik' class destroyer) Korv. Kap. Gerfried Brutzner

In Support: Wolfpack Gruppe Eisenbart

Controlled by Kapitän-zur-See Rudolf Peters, Fdu Norwegen (Narvik) ('Führer der U-boote Norwegen' [Commander, U-boat Forces, Norway], based in Narvik)

U-277 (Type VIIC U-boat) Kap. Lt. Robert Lübsen

U-314 (Type VIIC U-boat) Korv. Kap. Georg-Wilhelm Basse

U-354 (Type VIIC U-boat) Korv. Kap. Karl-Heinz Herbschleb

U-387 (Type VIIC U-boat) Korv. Kap. Rudolf Büchler

U-601 (Type VIIC U-boat) Kap. Lt. Otto Hansen

U-716 (Type VIIC U-boat) Ober. Lt. Hans Dunkelberg

U-957 (Type VIIC U-boat) Kap. Lt. Gerhard Schaar

The Battle of North Cape

The Royal Navy and its Allies
Note: this was not a purely Royal Naval effort – the forces at Admiral Fraser's disposal included four Canadian and one Norwegian destroyers, and a Norwegian corvette.

Elements of the Home Fleet Admiral Fraser

Force 1: Rear Admiral Burnett
HMS *Belfast* ('Edinburgh' class light cruiser) Flag of Rear Admiral Robert Burnett
Capt. Frederick Parham
HMS *Norfolk* ('Norfolk' class heavy cruiser) Capt. Donald Bain
HMS *Sheffield* ('Southampton' class light cruiser) Capt. Charles Addis

Force 2: Admiral Fraser
HMS *Duke of York* ('King George V' class battleship) Flag of Admiral Bruce Fraser
Capt. The Hon. Guy Russell
HMS *Jamaica* ('Fiji' class light cruiser) Capt. John Hughes-Hallett

36th Destroyer Division: Commander Fisher
Note: The division was attached to Convoy JW 55B, then to Force 1 and/or Force 2 as circumstances dictated.

71st Sub Division
HMS *Musketeer* ('L&M' class destroyer) Cdr. Ralph Fisher
HMS *Matchless* ('L&M' class destroyer) Lt. William Shaw

72nd Sub Division
HMS *Opportune* ('O&P' class destroyer) Cdr. John Lee-Barber
HMS *Virago* ('V' class destroyer) Lt. Cdr. Archibald White

1st Sub Division
HMS *Savage* ('S' class destroyer) Cdr. Michael Meyrick
HMS *Saumarez* ('S' class destroyer) Lt. Cdr. Eric Walmsley

2nd Sub Division
HMS *Scorpion* ('S' class destroyer) Lt. Cdr. William Clouston
HMNS *Stord* ('S' class destroyer) Lt. Cdr. Skule Storheill, RNN

Background

Convoy JW 55B (outward bound, from Loch Ewe to Murmansk)
Convoy Rear Admiral Maitland Boucher
19 Merchant Ships

Through Close Escort: Lt. Cdr. F.J.S. Hewitt
HMS *Gleaner* ('Halcyon' class minesweeper) Lt. Cdr. Frank Hewitt
HMS *Whitehall* (modified 'W' class destroyer) Lt. Cdr. Patrick Cowell
HMS *Wrestler* ('W' class destroyer) Lt. R.W.B. Lacon
HMS *Honeysuckle* ('Flower' class corvette) Lt. H.H.D. MacKilligan, RNR
HMS *Oxlip* ('Flower' class corvette) Lt. Cdr. C.W. Ledbetter, RNR

Fighting Destroyer Escort: Captain McCoy
HMS *Onslow* ('O&P' class destroyer) Capt. James McCoy
HMC *Haida* ('Tribal' class destroyer) Cdr. Henry de Wolf, RCN
HMC *Huron* ('Tribal' class destroyer) Lt. Cdr. Herbert Rayner, RCN
HMS *Impulsive* ('G, H & I' class destroyer) Lt. Cdr. P. Bekenn
HMCS *Iroquois* ('Tribal' class destroyer) Cdr. James 'Stumpy' Hibberd, RCN
HMS *Onslaught* ('O&P' class destroyer) Cdr. William Selby
HMS *Orwell* ('O&P' class destroyer) Lt. Cdr. John Hodges
HMS *Scourge* ('S' class destroyer) Lt. Cdr. George Balfour

Convoy RA 55A (homeward bound, from Murmansk to Loch Ewe)
22 Merchant Ships

Through Close Escort: Lt. Cdr. Ellis
HMS *Seagull* ('Halcyon' class minesweeper) Lt. Cdr. Richard Ellis
HMNoS *Andenes* ('Flower' class corvette) Lt. Cdr. E. Bruun, RNN
HMS *Dianella* ('Flower' class corvette) Lt. L.R.F. Tognola, RNR
HMS *Poppy* ('Flower' class corvette) Lt. Denzil Onslow, RNR

Fighting Destroyer Escort: Captain Campbell
HMS *Milne* ('L&M' class destroyer) Capt. Ian 'Scotty' Campbell
HMS *Ashanti* ('Tribal' class destroyer) Lt. Cdr. John Barnes
HMC *Athabaskan* ('Tribal' class destroyer) Cdr. John Stubbs, RCN

The Battle of North Cape

HMS *Beagle* ('A&B' class destroyer) Lt. Cdr. Norman Murch
HMS *Meteor* ('L&M' class destroyer) Lt. Cdr. Dermod Jewitt
HMS *Westcott* ('W' class destroyer) Lt. Cdr. Hedworth Lambton

Ship Specifications

The German Kriegsmarine

Class of vessel(s)	**'Scharnhorst' class battlecruiser**
Name of vessel(s)	*Scharnhorst*
Displacement	34,841 tons
Length	741 feet
Beam	98 feet
Draught	32½ feet
Armour	Belt, conning tower and main turrets: 14 inches. Armoured deck: 3 inches. Secondary turrets: 5½ inches
Armament	9 × 11-inch (280mm) guns in 3 triple turrets
	12 × 6-inch (150mm) guns in 4 twin and 4 single turrets
	14 × 4.1-inch (105mm) guns in 7 twin turrets
	16 × 37mm flak guns in 8 twin mounts
	32 × 20mm flak guns in single mounts
Speed	32 knots
Complement	1,840 men, 2 Arado seaplanes
Commissioned	1938
Class of vessel(s)	**Type 1936A 'Narvik' class destroyer**
Name of vessel(s)	*Z-29, Z-30, Z-33, Z-34* and *Z-36*
Displacement	*Z-29, Z-30*: 3,597 tons, *Z-33, Z-34* and *Z-36*: 2,603 tons
Length	400 feet
Beam	39 feet
Draught	13 feet
Armour	None
Armament	5 × 6-inch (150mm) guns in 1 twin turret (forward) and 3 single turrets
	2 × 37mm flak guns in twin mount
	10 × 20mm flak guns in 2 single and 2 quad mounts

Background

	8 × 21-inch (533mm) torpedo tubes, in 2 quadruple launchers
Speed	38½ knots
Complement	321 men
Commissioned	Z-29 and Z-30 commissioned 1940, Z-33 commissioned 1941, Z-34 and Z-36 commissioned 1942
Notes	Z-33, Z-34 and Z-36 were classified as 1936A (mob), standing for wartime mobilisation vessels, and were laid down during the war. The difference between the pre-war Z-29 and Z-30 vessels was virtually negligible – the earlier pair were initially fitted with a single rather than a twin 150mm gun turret forward, but in Z-29 this was replaced by a twin mount when it became available. Z-30 retained its single mount throughout the war. The pre-war vessels were also fitted with one extra twin 37mm flak mount, and carried just five 20mm flak guns, in single mounts

Class of vessel(s)	**Type VII C U-boat**
Name of vessel(s)	U-601, U-277, U-354, U-387, U-314, U-716 and U-957
Displacement	749 tons
Length	220 feet
Beam	20 feet
Draught	16 feet
Armament	1 × 88mm flak gun in single mount 5 × 21-inch (533mm) torpedo tubes, 4 in bows, 1 in stern (14 torpedoes carried)
Speed	17 knots on surface, 7½ knots submerged
Maximum depth	220 metres (722 feet)
Range	8,500 miles on surface, 80 miles when submerged (using battery power)
Complement	44 men
Commissioned	U-601 commissioned 1941, U-277, U-354 and U-387 commissioned 1942, U-314, U-716 and U-957 commissioned 1943

The Battle of North Cape

The Royal Navy and its Allies

Class of vessel(s)	**'King George V' class battleship**
Name of vessel(s)	HMS *Duke of York*
Displacement	36,727 tons
Length	700 feet
Beam	103 feet
Draught	32½ feet
Armour	Belt: 15 inches. Conning tower: 5½ inches. Main turrets: 13 inches. Deck: 6 inches
Armament	10 × 14-inch guns in 1 twin and 2 quadruple turrets
	16 × 5.2-inch guns in 8 twin turrets
	60 × 2-pdr anti-aircraft guns in 4 × 8-barrelled mounts
	38 × 20mm anti-aircraft guns in single mounts
	(2 Walrus seaplanes)
Speed	28 knots
Complement	1,422 men
Commissioned	1941
Class of vessel(s)	**'Norfolk' class heavy cruiser**
Name of vessel(s)	HMS *Norfolk*
Displacement	10,900 tons
Length	635 feet
Beam	66 feet
Draught	20 feet
Armour	Belt: 4 inches. Main turrets: 1 inch. Deck: unarmoured
Armament	8 × 8-inch guns in 4 twin turrets
	8 × 4-inch guns in 4 twin turrets
	16 × 2-pdr anti-aircraft guns in 2 × 8-barrelled mounts
	8 × 21-inch torpedoes in 2 quadruple launchers
Speed	32 knots
Complement	710 men
Commissioned	1930
Class of vessel(s)	**'Edinburgh' class light cruiser**
Name of vessel(s)	HMS *Belfast*

Background

Displacement	14,900 tons
Length	613 feet
Beam	66 feet
Draught	23 feet
Armour	Belt: 4½ inches. Main turrets: 4 inches. Deck: unarmoured
Armament	12 × 6-inch guns in 4 triple turrets
	12 × 4-inch guns in 6 twin turrets
	16 × 2-pdr anti-aircraft guns in 2 × 8-barrelled mounts
	6 × 21-inch torpedoes in 2 triple launchers
Speed	32½ knots
Complement	850 men
Commissioned	1939

Class of vessel(s)	**'Southampton' class light cruiser**
Name of vessel(s)	HMS *Sheffield*
Displacement	12,190 tons
Length	591 feet
Beam	62 feet
Draught	21½ feet
Armour	Belt: 4½ inches. Main turrets: 1 inch. Deck: unarmoured
Armament	12 × 6-inch guns in 4 triple turrets
	8 × 4-inch guns in 4 twin turrets
	8 × 2-pdr anti-aircraft guns in 2 quadruple mounts
	6 × 21-inch torpedoes in 2 triple launchers
Speed	32 knots
Complement	748 men
Commissioned	1937

Class of vessel(s)	**'Fiji' class light cruiser**
Name of vessel(s)	HMS *Jamaica*
Displacement	10,830 tons
Length	555½ feet
Beam	62 feet
Draught	20 feet

The Battle of North Cape

Armour	Belt: 3½ inches. Main turrets: 2 inches. Deck: unarmoured
Armament	12 × 6-inch guns in 4 triple turrets
	8 × 4-inch guns in 4 twin turrets
	8 × 2-pdr anti-aircraft guns in 2 quadruple mounts
	6 × 21-inch torpedoes in 2 triple launchers
Speed	31½ knots
Complement	920 men
Commissioned	1942

Class of vessel(s)	**'Tribal' class destroyer**
Name of vessel(s)	HMS *Ashanti*, HMC *Iroquois*, HMC *Athabaskan*, HMC *Haida*, *Huron*
Displacement	1,960 tons
Length	377 feet
Beam	36½ feet (37½ feet in Canadian destroyers)
Draught	13 feet
Armament	8 × 4.7-inch guns in 4 twin turrets
	4 × 2-pdr anti-aircraft guns in 1 quadruple mount
	4 × 21-inch torpedoes in 1 quadruple launcher
Speed	36½ knots
Complement	250 men
Commissioned	HMS *Ashanti* commissioned 1937, HMC *Iroquois* and *Athabaskan* commissioned 1941, HMC *Haida* and *Huron* commissioned 1942
Notes	HMC *Athabaskan* had only 6 × 4.7-inch guns, in 3 twin turrets

Class of vessel(s)	**'A&B' class destroyer/'G, H & I' class destroyer**
Name of vessel(s)	HMS *Beagle*, HMS *Impulsive*
Displacement	1,370 tons (1,360 tons for 'A&B' class)
Length	312 feet
Beam	32 feet
Draught	12 feet

Background

Armament	4 × 4.7-inch guns in 4 single turrets
	4 × 2-pdr anti-aircraft guns in 4 single mounts
	8 × 21-inch torpedoes in 2 quadruple launchers
Speed	36 knots (35½ knots for 'A&B' class)
Complement	145 men (138 for 'A&B' class)
Commissioned	HMS *Beagle* commissioned 1930, HMS *Impulsive* commissioned 1937
Notes	These two destroyer classes were similar, and shared the same basic characteristics. The more modern class was simply an improved version of the older one.

Class of vessel(s)	**'L&M' class destroyer**
Name of vessel(s)	HMS *Musketeer*, HMS *Meteor*, HMS *Milne* and HMS *Matchless*
Displacement	1,925 tons
Length	362 feet
Beam	37 feet
Draught	14½ feet
Armament	6 × 4.7-inch guns in 3 twin turrets
	4 × 2-pdr. anti-aircraft guns in 1 quadruple mount
	8 × 21-inch torpedoes in 2 quadruple launchers
Speed	36 knots
Complement	226 men
Commissioned	HMS *Musketeer*, HMS *Meteor*, HMS *Milne* and HMS *Matchless* commissioned 1941

Class of vessel(s)	**'O&P' class destroyer**
Name of vessel(s)	HMS *Onslaught*, HMS *Orwell* and HMS *Opportune*
Displacement	1,550 tons
Length	345 feet
Beam	35 feet
Draught	13½ feet
Armament	4 × 4.7-inch guns in 4 single turrets
	4 × 2-pdr. anti-aircraft guns in 1 quadruple mount
	8 × 21-inch torpedoes in 2 quadruple launchers

The Battle of North Cape

Speed	37 knots
Complement	212 men
Commissioned	HMS *Onslaught* commissioned 1941, HMS *Orwell* and HMS *Opportune* commissioned 1941

Class of vessel(s)	**'S' class destroyer/ 'V' class destroyer**
Name of vessel(s)	HMS *Saumarez*, HMS *Savage*, HMS *Scorpion*, HMS *Scourge*, HNMS *Stord*, HMS *Virago*
Displacement	1,730 tons
Length	363 feet
Beam	36 feet
Draught	14 feet
Armament	4 × 4.7-inch guns in 4 single turrets
	2 × 40mm Bofors anti-aircraft guns in 1 twin mount
	8 × 21-inch torpedoes in 2 quadruple launchers
Speed	37 knots
Complement	225 men
Commissioned	HMS *Saumarez*, HMS *Savage*, HMS *Scorpion* and HMS *Scourge* commissioned 1942, HNMS *Stord* commissioned 1943 as HMS *Success*, transferred to Royal Norwegian Navy later that year. HMS *Virago* commissioned 1943

Class of vessel(s)	**'W' class destroyer**
Name of vessel(s)	HMS *Wrestler*, HMS *Westcott* and HMS *Whitehall*
Displacement	1,100 tons (*Whitehall* was 1,325 tons)
Length	312 feet
Beam	31 feet
Draught	9½ feet
Armament	2 × 4-inch guns in 2 single turrets
	5 × 20mm anti-aircraft guns in 5 single mounts
	6 × 21-inch torpedoes in 2 triple launchers
Speed	25 knots
Complement	134 (127 men in HMS *Whitehall*)
Commissioned	HMS *Wrestler* and HMS *Westcott* commissioned 1918, HMS *Whitehall* commissioned 1919. All

Background

	were extensively modernised as long-range escorts in 1941
Notes	HMS *Whitehall* was a modified 'W' class, and was armed with 2 × 4.7-inch guns in 2 single turrets. The only real difference was her improved main armament

Class of vessel(s)	**'Halcyon' class minesweeper**
Name of vessel(s)	HMS *Gleaner* and HMS *Seagull*
Displacement	815 tons
Length	245½ feet
Beam	33½ feet
Draught	10 feet
Armament	2 × 4-inch guns in 2 single mounts
	4 × 20mm anti-aircraft guns in 4 single mounts
Speed	17 knots
Complement	80 men
Commissioned	HMS *Gleaner* and HMS *Seagull* commissioned 1918

Class of vessel(s)	**'Flower' class corvette**
Name of vessel(s)	HMS *Dianella*, HMS *Honeysuckle*, HMS *Oxlip*, HMS *Poppy* and HNMS *Andenes*
Displacement	1,170 tons
Length	205 feet
Beam	33 feet
Draught	14 feet
Armament	1 × 4-inch gun in 1 single mount
	1 × 2-pdr. anti-aircraft gun in 1 single mount
	2 × 20mm anti-aircraft guns in 2 single mounts (only on some corvettes)
Speed	16½ knots
Complement	109 men
Commissioned	HMS *Dianella* and HMS *Honeysuckle* commissioned 1941, HMS *Oxlip* and HMS *Poppy* commissioned 1942. HMNoS *Andenes* commissioned 1942 as HMS *Acanthus*, transferred to Royal Norwegian Navy later that year

Campaign
Chronicle

⊳━━━━━⊸•(•)•⊷━━━━━⊲

Day 1: Monday, 20 December 1943

Seconds before 17:00 hours, Rear Admiral Maitland Boucher gave the order. A signal gun fired, its smoke whipped away by the strong southeasterly wind, and the flag signal for 'Convoy shall proceed' was hoisted above the *Fort Kullyspell*, which served as the admiral's flagship. The large, ponderous screws of nineteen merchant ships began to turn, and Convoy JW 55B got under way. Named after a Canadian trading post, the *Fort Kullyspell* was typical of the ships that made up the rest of the convoy. She was a brand new merchantman – a 'Victory Ship' – built at the West Coast Shipbuilders' Yard at Vancouver, and handed over to her new owners just four months earlier. Technically, the Canadian-built merchantman was owned by the Hall Brothers Shipping Company of Newcastle, Canada, but 'for the duration' she was operated on behalf of the Ministry of War Transport. Like other 'Victory Ships' of the 'Fort' class she was 441 feet in length and distinguished by having a single funnel, a central island superstructure, and hatch spaces with cranes (derricks) fore and aft. On paper she displaced some 7,192 tons, although that morning, with her holds filled with crated aircraft and stores, she rode considerably lower in the water than usual.

Convoy JW 55B had gathered at the head of Loch Ewe, a deepwater inlet some 10 miles long and 4 miles wide at its broadest point, just south of the Isle of Ewe. It was a remote spot, fringed with little

22

Day 1: Monday, 20 December 1943

hamlets, the largest of which was Poolewe. It was a beautiful, tranquil spot – if you liked that sort of thing. For the sailors on board the merchantmen and escort vessels it was idyllic, compared with where they were going. It took the best part of an hour for the gaggle of ships to pass the headland of Rubha na Sasan and enter the open Atlantic waters of The Minches. Nowadays, a solitary monument stands on that lonely, chilly headland, but in December 1943 it was garrisoned, and the convoy was watched by the bored, benumbed, men of the Artillery Regiment. Their job was to guard the entrance to the great sea loch. Gun emplacements, boom nets and anti-aircraft positions all played their part in turning this part of the West Coast of Scotland into one of the most important anchorages in Europe.

Once out in The Minches the ships turned to starboard and headed north-north-east, with the mainland of Scotland on their starboard side and the Isle of Lewis somewhere through the wintry darkness to port. By midnight the convoy was passing the shelter of the Butt of Lewis, the northern tip of the island, while Cape Wrath – the north-western tip of the Scottish mainland – lay 10 miles to starboard. The merchantmen and their escorts now began to feel the full force of the Atlantic swell as the ships steamed on through the darkness. The night of 21/22 December would prove uneventful – just the first leg of a long, cold, dangerous voyage.

Some 300 miles to the north, another group of ships was making preparations to put to sea. The Fighting Destroyer Escort, made up of ships from the 17th Destroyer Flotilla lying in the Skaalefjord (Skálafjordur) off Tórshavn, the capital of the Faeroe Islands, where their crews were taking on stores. Captain 'Bes' McCoy's flotilla was Convoy JW 55B's covering force, and its departure was scheduled to coincide with the arrival of the convoy at a rendezvous 64 degrees north – due north of the Faeroes and east of Iceland. The sailing of JW 55B had already been delayed twenty-four hours due to bad weather, so McCoy's men had a day's respite. If all went according to plan the destroyers would sail late the following evening.

Approximately 700 miles to the north-north-west Admiral Fraser's Force 2 was heading back to Akureyri on the Eyjafjördur, its bleak anchorage on Iceland's northern coast, having just escorted the previous Convoy JW 55A all the way to the Kola Inlet. The flagship *Duke of York* was expected to arrive at Akureyri late the following evening.

The Battle of North Cape

The force would then take on fuel and stores and return to sea forty-eight hours later, where it would provide long-range cover for Convoy JW 55B.

The final two elements in this giant operation were approximately 1,500 miles away from the *Fort Kullyspell*, lying in the desolate Soviet anchorage of the Kola Inlet. The nineteen merchantmen of Convoy JW 55A had reached the anchorage the evening before – late on 19 December, escorted by a force of Royal Navy cruisers. Kola Inlet was home to the Soviet Northern Fleet, and led to the port of Murmansk, where a railway ran south into the heart of Russia. Rear Admiral Burnett's Force 1 had reached its designated anchorage at Vaenga Bay just after midnight that morning – 20 December. The British warship anchorage was close but separate from the main Soviet naval base at Polyarni Inlet, which lay on the opposite side of the great waterway. 20 December was spent refuelling, as Force 1 prepared to put to sea again.

That afternoon a Convoy Conference was held on board the light cruiser *Belfast*, which served as Burnett's flagship. It was attended by the admiral, the convoy commodore, their respective staffs, and by the captains and masters of all the warships and merchantmen who were destined to take part in the forthcoming operation. Outgoing Convoy JW 55A had reached port safely but, given the limited cargo handling facilities available, it would take up to four weeks to unload all its stores. Therefore, the homeward bound convoy – designated RA 55A – consisted of merchant ships that had already spent some time in the inlet, anchored at Rosta, halfway between Vaenga Bay and Murmansk, on the exposed eastern side of the waterway. Seven lucky ships had arrived as part of JW 54B, and therefore had spent just seventeen days at Kola. The rest had arrived there almost four weeks before, as part of Convoy JW 54A. The captains involved must have been delighted to know they were finally heading home. The aim of the conference was to sort out any problems, talk strategy and tactics, and make sure everyone knew what to do. As Convoy JW 55B was steaming out of Loch Ewe, the Convoy Conference on board *Belfast* broke up and Burnett and his officers prepared for their evening's entertainment – a concert by the Soviet Red Banner Fleet Choir.

These five elements – the two convoys, the two covering forces, and the destroyer escort – were all vital parts in a colossal naval operation.

Day 1: Monday, 20 December 1943

When Rear Admiral Boucher ordered Convoy JW 55B to put to sea he started this operation in train, and like a well-oiled machine every constituent part – every warship and merchantman – had a particular role to play. Each ship was assigned a station and given orders to follow. Each naval force had particular roles within the overall task of screening the two convoys. Given the limitations and vagaries of naval communications, every group of ships was operating to a timetable, its scheduled day and time of sailing designed to tie in with the movements of all the other groups. In fact, the whole operation was choreographed like an intricate dance, and if all went well the performance would end in success. However, much could go wrong: the weather was deteriorating and meteorological reports predicted that by Christmas Day the operational area off the northern coast of Norway would be battered by a gale that could reach Storm Force 11. Given the number of ships involved the chances of mechanical failure were high, while senior naval commanders knew from bitter experience just how difficult it could be to control a multi-national convoy, whose merchant ships were commanded by independent-minded masters.

Then there were the Germans. Of all the variables that could influence the outcome of the operation, the enemy was the most unpredictable. The Germans maintained a screen of U-boats across the path of the Arctic convoys, patrolling between the southern limit of the Arctic ice pack and the Norwegian coast near North Cape. German reconnaissance aircraft covered much of the Norwegian Sea and Barents Sea, making it likely that Allied naval movements would be spotted and reported to the German Naval High Command.

Finally there was the *Scharnhorst*, lurking in the Altenfjord, and waiting to pounce. Together with her escort of modern destroyers, she represented a powerful fighting force – more than a match for the cruisers of Force 1, and fast enough to outpace the battleship that formed the backbone of Force 2. Given the deteriorating weather – and a dose of luck – the Germans could pounce on Convoy JW 55B or even RA 55A before the covering forces could react.

Orchestrating this great naval operation was Admiral Bruce Fraser, who flew his flag in the battleship *Duke of York*. The battleship constituted his floating headquarters, where intelligence was gathered, positions plotted and orders issued. While he remained in control of the operation, the real masterminds were entombed in an underground

The Battle of North Cape

concrete bunker beneath the Admiralty Building in London's Whitehall. They gathered every scrap of information, including reports from all the warships involved, British submarines on patrol off the Altenfjord, Norwegian resistance agents, and the aircraft of Coastal Command, the Fleet Air Arm and the Royal Air Force. Above all, they gathered German radio intercepts, much of which could be decoded thanks to a major British intelligence breakthrough.

German naval signals were broadcast after being passed through an Enigma machine, a mechanical computer that turned the signal into a code the Germans considered unbreakable. In May 1941 the British captured an Enigma machine for themselves and managed to keep their acquisition a secret from the Germans. By late 1943 the majority of German naval signals were being intercepted and decoded by British Naval Intelligence, and consequently the Admiralty had information of German naval movements almost as quickly as their counterparts in the German Naval High Command. Codenamed 'Ultra', this intelligence source gave the Allies a significant edge over the Germans. When the Admiralty deemed it important, then details of these 'Ultra' signal intercepts were passed to Admiral Fraser and his staff. These would allow him to know when the *Scharnhorst* put to sea, and therefore would give him a better chance of placing his warships between the Germans and the convoys.

That evening, as the *Duke of York* passed Jan Mayen Island heading towards Iceland, 650 miles to the west another admiral was holding a meeting with his staff on board his flagship. They discussed the latest batch of signals from patrolling U-boats, and the implications of a dramatic statement made by the head of the German Navy earlier that day. Konter-Admiral Erich Bey was a destroyer commander at heart, but less than six weeks before, on 9 November, he had assumed command of the Kriegsmarine's Battlegroup stationed in the Altenfjord. In effect, this meant he commanded the battlecruiser *Scharnhorst* and her escort group of five destroyers, although his flagship remained the disabled *Tirpitz*, anchored in the Kåfjord, the southern arm of the Altenfjord. A week after assuming command his Staff Office on the *Tirpitz* received a report that an enemy convoy was passing Bear Island, and he put the *Scharnhorst* on three hours' notice for sailing.

The only German forces at sea at the time were the U-boats of Gruppe Eisenbart, commanded by Kapitän-zur-See Rudolf Peters

Day 1: Monday, 20 December 1943

from his shore base in Narvik. Somehow this convoy – JW 54A – had managed to evade all German U-boats, reaching the Kola Inlet without incident (the bulk of these merchant ships would later form the core of Convoy RA 55A). However, Peters had a bunch of good excuses: he only had four operational submarines at his disposal, the seas were rough, and during the short hours of daylight visibility was extremely limited. His screen was little more than a token, and it would only be with great luck that his U-boats would be able to detect, let alone attack, an enemy convoy. As Peters put it in his diary on 7 December: 'I have to acknowledge that surveillance of the Bear Island Gap is not practicable with the means at my disposal.' However, the failure to attack the convoy rankled with Kapitän-zur-See Rolf Johannesson, commanding the five operational destroyers of the 4th Destroyer Flotilla. He wrote: 'The 17th of November 1943 is a day that deserves to be remembered. That was the day we relinquished all initiative in the war, and went on to the defensive as far as surface vessels are concerned.' He was wrong: a month later Johannesson and his destroyers would be committed to the attack.

Although the sortie against JW 54A never happened, the fuel tanks of the German battlecruiser had been topped up and her commander, Kapitän-zur-See Fritz Hintze, felt it was a pity to waste the opportunity this presented. Therefore, on 25 November he took the *Scharnhorst* out to sea to test her engines. The tests proved highly successful and the *Scharnhorst* returned to her usual lair in the Langefjord, a western arm of the Altenfjord. He repeated the sortie on 14 December, taking the *Scharnhorst* round to the Burfjord just outside the mouth of the Altenfjord. Early on 19 December, as the *Scharnhorst* returned to her old mooring in the Langefjord, Peters in Narvik sent the admiral news of a fresh convoy sighting. The day before, *U-636* sent a confusing report suggesting that an enemy ship had been spotted in the Barents Sea. That night the commander of *U-354* reported seeing star shells on the horizon. It was becoming clear that another convoy had slipped past the Germans and reached the safety of the Kola Inlet.

Having missed Convoy JW 55A, Bey must have felt the pressure mounting. After all, the reason his Battlegroup remained at readiness was to launch an attack against an enemy convoy. He had known since 18 November that the Allies had resumed their Arctic convoys, and he knew that it was inevitable that he would be ordered to attack the next one, regardless of the odds against him. On 19 December the head of the Kriegsmarine, Grossadmiral Karl Dönitz, flew to the 'Wolfsschanze' ('Wolf's Lair'), Hitler's operational headquarters at Rastenberg in East Prussia. He was there to take part in a two-day Führer Conference, where Hitler and his senior commanders discussed strategy. Fearing his political position would be undermined, Dönitz reported that the Arctic convoys had resumed, and that the *Scharnhorst* and her escorts would attack the next outward-bound convoy if a favourable opportunity presented itself. As he spoke, Convoy JW 55B was preparing to sail from Loch Ewe – the fourth such convoy in five weeks. This time there would be no hesitation: the honour of the German surface fleet would be redeemed by a daring strike, and the *Scharnhorst* would finally sortie in earnest.

Day 2: Tuesday, 21 December 1943

Dawn found Convoy JW 55B to the west of Orkney, still heading north-north-east in a lumpy swell. The ships were scattered over several miles, as the station-keeping abilities of several of the merchant captains was less than naval in its precision. At 08:00 hours Rear Admiral Boucher gave the order to adopt the approved convoy formation, and while the admiral's yeomen bombarded their charges with radio messages and flag signals, the escorts began the tiresome business of shepherding wayward charges into their assigned position.

The convoy was arranged in six columns, each a nautical mile apart, with between two and four ships in each column. In theory the merchantmen in each of these columns kept half a nautical mile apart. The *Fort Kullyspell* was the lead ship of Column 3, in the centre of the convoy, while the Deputy Convoy Commander in the *Fort Nakasley* took station at the head of Column 1. The Assistant Convoy Commander and his small staff were on board the *Ocean Pride*, the middle ship in Column 5. Probably the most vulnerable ship in the convoy was the *Norlys*, a 9,900-ton tanker, built in Hamburg, but which now flew a Panamanian flag. Boucher tucked her in the centre of the convoy, behind his own flagship. This meant that Convoy JW 55B was spread over some 5 miles of ocean, stretching for a mile and a half astern of the flagship. Speed was increased to 9½ knots –

Diagram 1: The Deployment of Convoy JW 55B

Column 1	Column 2	Column 3	Column 4	Column 5	Column 6
Fort Nakasley (UK)	*Bernard N. Baker* (US)	*Fort Kullyspell* (UK)	*Thomas U. Walter* (US)	*Harold L. Winslow* (US)	*Ocean Viceroy* (UK)
Ocean Valour (UK)	*Fort Vercheres* (UK)	*Norlys* (Panamanian)	*British Statesman* (UK)	*Ocean Pride* (UK)	*Will Rogers* (US)
John J. Abel (US)	*Cardinal Gibbons* (US)	*Brockholst Livingston* (US)	*Ocean Messenger* (UK)	*Ocean Gypsy* (UK)	
	John Wanamaker (US)	*John Vining* (US)			

Note: For the purposes of the diagram 'UK' also includes ships from the British Commonwealth.

virtually top speed for what was rated a 'Fast Convoy' – defined as a force capable of making 10 knots.

These nineteen merchantmen were escorted by two groups of warships – the 'Local Escort' and the 'Through Escort'. The Local Escort consisted of just two small 'Flower' class corvettes – HMS *Borage* and HMS *Wallflower*, accompanied by the 'Algerine' class minesweeper HMS *Hound* (Senior Officer). A second minesweeper – HMS *Hydra* – had missed the sailing of the convoy due to mechanical problems, and would endeavour to catch up later. These four little warships were supposed to escort the convoy as far as the latitude of 64° North – the same latitude as Reykjavik in Iceland – before returning home to Loch Ewe. The Through Escort, which formed part of the Western Approaches Command was – as the name suggests – charged with accompanying the convoy all the way from Loch Ewe to the Kola Inlet. It was commanded by Lt. Cdr. Hewitt, who flew his flag in the 'Halcyon' class minesweeper HMS *Gleaner*. He also commanded two 'V&W' class destroyers, HMS *Whitehall* and HMS *Wrestler*, and the 'Flower' class corvettes HMS *Honeysuckle* and HMS *Oxlip*. These two groups constituted a powerful enough force to keep enemy U-boats at bay, but they were completely outclassed by the modern German destroyers at Altenfjord, and offered no form of deterrent whatsoever to the *Scharnhorst*.

Throughout the day, Rear Admiral Boucher conducted exercises, designed to instil a modicum of naval discipline among his mercantile charges. Emergency turns out of formation, lifeboat and firefighting drills, and the firing of anti-aircraft weapons were all practised by merchant ships and warships alike, until the convoy commander was satisfied the merchant captains understood the basics of what was expected of them in Arctic waters. For much of the day the convoy enjoyed the protection of air cover, provided by fighters from Twatt aerodrome in Orkney. Meanwhile, long-range Sunderland flying boats flew ahead of its path, keeping a watchful eye for signs of U-boats. So far everything had gone smoothly, although Boucher was a little worried about the station-keeping abilities of some of his merchant crews.

At 04:40 hours Force 2 made landfall on the north coast of Iceland, and an hour later the *Duke of York* entered the 120-mile long Eyjafjördur, which led to the anchorage at Akureyri. According to

Day 2: Tuesday, 21 December 1943

Lt. Cdr. Courage, on Admiral Fraser's staff, the traverse of the fjord was conducted 'at full speed in single line ahead, up a long inlet in very poor visibility – so poor that it was a job for the destroyers to see the next ahead'. This was more than sheer bravado – the *Duke of York*, at the head of the column, was using her radar as a navigation aid – Fraser was simply using the passage of the fjord as an exercise in building the Force's confidence in manoeuvres using radar. The value of this lesson would be demonstrated five days later. However, as Courage put it, 'the ships following astern of us were amazed and somewhat frightened by the speed at which we entered these hazardous waters'.

By noon, Force 2 was safely at anchor off Akureyri, and Fraser sent a signal to all his ships, assuring them that Convoy JW ˙55A had arrived safely in the Kola Inlet. He also had a message piped around his flagship, thanking its crew for making their recent visit to Russia a diplomatic success. Of course, Fraser was pleased for other reasons. As he put it in his diary:

> With the safe arrival of JW 55A I felt very strongly that the *Scharnhorst* would come out and endeavour to attack JW 55B. Fortunately my small force had now been in company for nearly a fortnight, we knew each other, and had practised night encounter tactics together.

The British admiral was more than happy to use the merchantmen of Convoy JW 55B as the bait that would lure the German battlecruiser out of her lair.

As for the crew of the *Scharnhorst*, the day passed quietly. Admiral Bey had ordered reconnaissance flights to search the Norwegian and Barents Seas for signs of another convoy, but the storm had grounded all flights from the German airfields in northern Norway. However, just after 16:00 hours he ordered his Battlegroup – the *Scharnhorst* and her five attendant destroyers – to go to six hours' notice for sea. Mail came on board – probably the last batch to arrive before Christmas. Strangely enough, some eighty crewmen also left the ship, having been granted Christmas leave. They were the lucky ones, heading back to Germany for three weeks while their shipmates remained in the bleak confines of the Langefjord. Although Kapitän-zur-See

The Battle of North Cape

Hintze knew that his battlecruiser would be making a sortie some time in the next few weeks, the essential domestic routine of the warship continued. Those leave-takers knew they might miss the action, but loyalty to their shipmates was countered by the excitement of seeing their families.

The Fighting Destroyer Escort sailed from the Skaalefjord (Skálafjordur), in the Faeroe Islands, at 23:45 hours, heading north on a course to rendezvous with Convoy JW 55B late the following day. Captain J.A. 'Bes' McCoy had eight destroyers under his command – the entire 17th Destroyer Flotilla. Apart from his flagship, the 'O&P' class destroyer HMS *Onslow*, McCoy's flotilla included two other vessels in the same class, HMS *Onslaught* and HMS *Orwell*. He also commanded the older 'I' class destroyer, HMS *Impulsive* and the 'S&T' class vessel, HMS *Scourge*, as well as three Canadian 'Tribal' class destroyers – HMCS *Iroquois*, HMCS *Haida* and HMCS *Huron*. The job of the Fighting Destroyer Escort was to provide anti-surface-ship protection for the convoy. In other words, whether it was attacked by destroyers or by the *Scharnhorst*, McCoy and his crews were expected to engage the enemy in an effort to protect the convoy.

Far to the east, in the Kola Inlet, preparations were well under way for the sailing of Convoy RA 55A. The merchant ships had been prepared for sea, their captains had been briefed, and where appropriate, naval convoy detachments had arrived on board to help with station-keeping and emergencies. In Vaenga Bay the crews of the cruisers *Belfast*, *Norfolk* and *Sheffield* made the most of a quiet day, completing the refuelling and taking on of stores. The plan called for them to sail in company with the homeward bound convoy on 23 December, which gave the men forty-eight hours of respite from the winter gales of the Barents Sea. However, not everyone was happy on board the *Belfast*. The midshipmen's gunroom was still recovering from the aftermath of the concerts provided by the Soviet Red Banner Fleet Choir the night before. The gunroom had been used as a dressing room, and when the Russian sailors left the midshipmen found the cabin had been comprehensively looted by their visitors. Sensibly enough, Captain Parham of the *Belfast* decided not to make a formal complaint to the Russian authorities – the unfortunate midshipmen were told to chalk the incident up to experience.

Day 3: Wednesday, 22 December 1943

Day 3: Wednesday, 22 December 1943

At 08:00 hours on the morning of 22 December, Convoy JW 55B was some 60 miles north-north-east of the Faeroe Islands, heading on a compass course of 017°. That put it some 400 miles west of German-occupied Norway, the nearest landfall being the port of Ålesund, close to the small German air base near Åndalsnes. That also put it within range of another airfield at Sola, just outside Stavanger, which was used by long-range maritime reconnaissance aircraft. However, Rear Admiral Boucher had more immediate problems than the possibility of being spotted by the Germans. During the night, the convoy had altered course by 15° to starboard, but the merchant ships *Ocean Valour* and *J. John Abel* somehow failed to make the course change and continued on their old course. They were the last two ships of Column 1, on the port side of the convoy. Boucher realised that in six hours they could be up to 13 miles to the west of the rest of the convoy, so he sent HMS *Whitehall* to round up the two merchant ships, which were escorted back into position.

While this was going on, the speed of the convoy was reduced slightly to 8 knots, to give the stragglers a chance to catch up. Then, at 09:20 hours, the minesweeper HMS *Hydra* caught up with the convoy, her departure from Loch Ewe having been delayed by engine problems. JW 55B was now outside the range of fighter aircraft based in Orkney or Shetland, but the long-range aircraft of Coastal Command could still reach its position. At 10.10 hours a Sunderland flying boat arrived, and swept ahead of the convoy on an anti-submarine patrol. Twenty minutes later it returned and exchanged signals with HMS *Hound* at the head of the convoy before heading home. It reported that no U-boats had been spotted and noted the convoy's position.

Just thirty minutes later, at 11:00 hours, the lookouts on board the minesweeper, HMS *Gleaner*, again heard the sound of an aircraft and at first they presumed it was the Sunderland, back for another look around. The *Gleaner* was on the starboard beam of the convoy, and the sound of the aircraft came from astern of them. Then they saw the aircraft – a German bomber. It was heading due east, no doubt returning to base after a reconnaissance flight. Lieutenant Commander Hewitt signalled the news to the *Fort Kullyspell*. Rear Admiral Boucher had to assume that the convoy had been spotted and that details of its position would be passed on to Admiral Bey.

In fact, the aircraft was a twin-engined Junkers 88 light bomber, on a routine patrol gathering meteorological information. This weather plane had indeed spotted the convoy, several minutes before it was spotted by the lookouts on the minesweeper. The Junkers was already heading back to its base at Værnes, outside Trondheim, when it came across the convoy, and the crew immediately radioed the news to their base. The brief glimpses these airmen had of the convoy through the low cloud cover led them to greatly overestimate its size and even its composition. The signal read: 'At 10:45, in Square AE6983: 40 troop-ships and escort vessels, probably with Aircraft Carrier. Course 045°, Speed 10 knots.' The only accurate part of the report was the location of the convoy and its approximate speed.

Around noon, the report was passed from the Luftwaffe head-quarters in northern Norway to German Naval Headquarters in Kiel, where it was handed to Generaladmiral Otto Schniewind, who was Bey's nominal superior. Schniewind was sceptical, writing in his diary that 'I incline to the view that there are many sources of error attached to a (report from a) weather plane'. Despite his reservations, he passed the report on to Admiral Bey, as well as the U-boat base in Narvik. The sighting placed the convoy around 64° north, 6° west, on a reported course that would have the force making landfall in northern Norway, possibly at Narvik. Adolf Hitler had long been convinced the Allies would try to recapture Norway, and as the report stood, this seemed to suggest he was right. A force of forty troopships could contain an overwhelming military force, and this appeared to be an invasion fleet rather than a convoy.

The Germans reacted accordingly. The U-boats of the Eisenbart group were ordered south from their patrol lines in the Barents Sea to cover the entrance to the Vestfjord, the 25-mile wide channel leading towards Narvik. Despite the bad weather, the Luftwaffe was ordered to make visual contact with the convoy and to search the area within 300 miles of the Allied force, in order to locate other naval formations. After all, an invasion fleet would need covering aircraft carriers and battleships to help counter the threat posed by the *Scharnhorst*. Admiral Bey was ordered to take his ships to three hours' notice, a

Day 3: Wednesday, 22 December 1943

signal which reached him while he was visiting the *Scharnhorst*. Less than an hour later, Kapitän-zur-See Hintze reported his ship ready.

The invasion threat passed almost as quickly as it arrived. When the weather plane landed at Værnes, just before 13:00 hours, the crewmen were debriefed by the squadron intelligence officer. It turned out they had only a few fleeting glimpses of the ships below them, and from their description of the formation they had seen, it soon became apparent that their report had been both inaccurate and exaggerated. At 14:30 hours a new signal was sent, informing recipients to 'delete troop transports' and replace the phrase with references to merchant ships. It added that the 'visual reconnaissance was unreliable owing to poor visibility'. In other words, the Luftwaffe had got it badly wrong. In Kiel, Generaladmiral Schniewind ordered the U-boats of the Eisenbart group to return to their old patrol line. However, the request for additional air reconnaissance remained in effect, while the *Scharnhorst* and her five escorts still waited at three hours' notice.

At noon Rear Admiral Boucher sent a routine situation report to the Admiralty, which told of steadily worsening weather and poor visibility. The strength of the wind had been increasing all morning, the beginning of the strong southwesterly gale, which had been forecast by the Admiralty. Still, Boucher was lucky – the outer bands of the storm had grounded German reconnaissance flights from Norwegian airfields for the past three days, and despite his encounter with the weather plane that morning, he knew that a storm would provide perfect cover for his convoy, however unpleasant it might make the voyage. He also expected to rendezvous with the Fighting Destroyer Escort some time that afternoon and would therefore be a little less vulnerable to attack.

At 13:15 hours another Sunderland flying boat passed over the convoy from the south, signalling the escort commander on board HMS *Hound*, who passed news of an approaching force to the *Fort Kullyspell*. Some fifty minutes earlier it had flown over Captain McCoy's Fighting Destroyer Escort and the convoy commander was duly told that his reinforcements were 25 miles away to the south, on a bearing of 172°. In fact, McCoy had altered course to due north, and increased speed to 18 knots. He knew that meeting a convoy in bad weather was a tricky business and errors in navigation and station-keeping could prove disastrous. Consequently, he planned to take station before the weather got any worse.

McCoy spread his ships out into line abreast, each destroyer 2 miles from its neighbour. That gave him a search area of approximately 12 miles, increasing his chances of making contact regardless of visibility. His destroyers were also fitted with basic radar sets, which greatly increased his chances of picking up the convoy. At 14:00 hours Commander Selby in HMS *Onslaught* reported contact – his lookouts had spotted the stern of the *Ocean Gypsy*, the rearmost merchant ship of Column 5, on the starboard side of the convoy. The *Onslaught* was the second destroyer from the port end of McCoy's line, and the merchant ship lay on a bearing of 027°, which effectively placed the convoy dead ahead of McCoy's force. The 'convoy meet' had been accomplished successfully and within an hour the eight destroyers had taken up formation ahead of, and on the flanks of, JW 55B. At 15:00 hours McCoy duly took over the role of Senior Escort Commander and on his signal, HMS *Hound* and the other three Local Escort vessels detached themselves from the convoy and set a course for the Skaalefjord (Skálafjordur) in the Faeroe Islands.

The news that the convoy had been spotted, and that the 'convoy meet' was successful, was passed to Admiral Fraser that afternoon. The *Duke of York* was anchored off Akureyri, where the battleship, along with the cruiser *Jamaica* and their escorting destroyers were all busy taking on board fuel from the tanker stationed in the fjord. Fraser knew that Convoy JW 55B was dangerously exposed to enemy attack, but then, that was exactly what he wanted. To him, the convoy was the bait, which – with luck – would tempt the *Scharnhorst* out to sea. Once she launched an attack against the convoy, Fraser was certain he would be able to intercept and damage the German battlecruiser, if not destroy her completely. It was a calculated risk, the mid-game of a nautical chess match played between Fraser and Bey.

While Admiral Fraser was having lunch on board his flagship off Akureyri, and Captain McCoy's destroyers were taking position around Convoy JW 55B, Admiral Bey had just sailed up the Altenfjord and the Langefjord on board *R-12*, a small coastal minesweeper. The 40-mile journey from the anchorage of the *Tirpitz* in the Kåfjord to that of the *Scharnhorst* near the head of the Langefjord took the

Day 3: Wednesday, 22 December 1943

admiral almost two and a half hours, but it was well worth the effort. It was a pre-Christmas visit, and the admiral and his staff brought mail and extra rations, as well as Christmas 'comforts' knitted by the womenfolk of Germany. This kind of morale-raising visit was important after the *Scharnhorst* had effectively spent a week at short notice for sea. Konter-Admiral Bey arrived on board at 11:30 hours and accompanied Kapitän-zur-See Hintze on his captain's rounds, the two men distributing goods to the crew as they progressed through the ship.

The admiral stayed for lunch – a guest of the *Scharnhorst*'s wardroom – and while the ship's company settled down to open their mail, the officers dined in as much style as they could manage, given the circumstances. However, as Bey was about to depart again, a signal arrived, forwarded by the admiral's office on board the *Tirpitz*. It was the order to go to three hours' notice. The signal had been sent by Admiral Nordmann, who was in charge of North Sea operations and who, in this case, acted as a signals intermediary between Admiral Bey and the office of the chief of the Navy in Kiel. Hintze gave the necessary orders, while the admiral and the senior officers of the battlecruiser met to consider the implications of this new development. The signal had been accompanied by a copy of the report from the weather plane and Bey remained sceptical. Both he and Hintze thought it more likely that the airmen had spotted an Arctic convoy rather than an invasion force.

Kapitän-zur-See Rolf Johannesson of the 4th Destroyer Flotilla had also been invited on board the *Scharnhorst* for lunch, and so, while the signal was passed to his five destroyers, he was able to discuss with Bey and Hintze the likelihood of a sortie. As soon as he could, Johannesson made his excuses and returned to his flagship, the destroyer Z29, which was anchored midway up the Langefjord. There his flag officer, Korvettenkapitän von Mutius, had already brought the destroyers to readiness. The two officers held their own discussion, working out the best way to attack a convoy. As Johannesson put it: 'there was no Christmas for Mutius and myself. We spent it plotting the convoy in my cabin.'

By the time Admiral Bey had returned to the *Tirpitz* later that afternoon, the clarification of the report by the weather plane had reached his flagship. While confirmation that the Allied force wasn't planning

The Battle of North Cape

an invasion was good news, it confirmed there was a convoy out there, waiting to be attacked. The statement by Grossadmiral Dönitz to Adolf Hitler in the 'Wolfsschanze' left Bey in no doubt that his force was expected to sortie and attack the convoy. Anything else would be a serious loss of face for the Kriegsmarine. The implications for the surface fleet were serious: a failure could lead to a directive to dismantle the fleet and to use what resources remained in other ways. That evening Bey and his staff knew exactly what was at stake.

What Konter-Admiral Bey didn't know was that there wasn't just one Arctic convoy at sea that evening. Convoy RA 55A sailed from the Kola Inlet during the late afternoon – twenty-three merchant ships, including eleven American merchantmen and one Dutch vessel, and escorted by two groups of warships. The first of these was the Through Close Escort, commanded by Lt. Cdr. Ellis in the minesweeper HMS *Seagull*. The rest of his force consisted of three 'Flower' class corvettes – HMS *Dianella*, HMS *Poppy* and HMNoS *Andenes* (formerly HMS *Acanthus*), of the Royal Norwegian Navy. Then there was Captain Ian Campbell's Fighting Destroyer Escort, made up of six warships from Campbell's own 3rd Destroyer Flotilla. Campbell flew his flag as Senior Escort Commander in the 'L/M' class destroyer HMS *Milne*. The rest of his flotilla consisted of the destroyers HMS *Ashanti* ('Tribal' class), HMS *Beagle* ('B' class), HMS *Meteor* ('L/M' class) and HMS *Westcott* ('V/W' class) and the Canadian destroyer HMC *Athabaskan* ('Tribal' class).

Rear Admiral Burnett's Force 1 remained in the Kola Inlet for another night, and that evening he and his officers attended a farewell reception hosted by Admiral Golovko, the Soviet Port Commander at Murmansk and the Kola Inlet. Captain Parham of the *Belfast* described the reception as an occasion when 'we drank vodka and ate stinking fish'. However, it was clear that Admiral Golovko was trying to overcome past suspicion and distrust between the Allies – as the evening wound to a close, he presented Admiral Burnett with a young reindeer named Olga. The *Belfast*'s new mascot was housed in the empty hangar – the Walrus seaplane had been left behind in Orkney a few months before – which made a perfect reindeer crèche. Burnett planned to sail early the following morning. His force could easily catch up with the convoy, and besides, sailing in two groups might help confuse enemy intelligence.

Day 4: Thursday, 23 December 1943

The scene was now set: two convoys were approaching the waters of northern Norway, one from the east, the other from the south-west. The existence of one was known to the Germans, but not the other. These two convoys were protected by two British naval forces, one of which was about to enter the waters of the Barents Sea from the east, the other from the west. Although Konter-Admiral Bey suspected these forces might be at large, he knew nothing of their strength or location. Then there was the string of U-boats, heading back into the waters of the Barents Sea after being called south to protect the sea approaches to Narvik. The final piece in this naval chess game was the German Battlegroup, still lurking in the Altenfjord, just waiting for enough information on enemy movements to ensure they could launch a successful attack against Convoy JW 55B. Everything was now in place for a showdown that would decide the fate of the convoy and the German surface navy.

Day 4: Thursday, 23 December 1943

It was a very cold night in Norway – temperatures were so far below freezing that when dawn broke, the head of the Eyjafjördur had frozen and much of the salt water anchorage at Akureyri was covered in a layer of ice. The sea between the *Duke of York* and the shore had frozen over, and the ice was solid enough for the crew to clamber down and walk around. The destroyers attached to the force spent the morning refuelling, while on board the battleship Admiral Fraser and his staff pored over the latest intelligence reports, and planned their next move. The admiral knew that Convoy JW 55B had been spotted by the Germans, but he was determined to stick to his original plan. The convoy would continue on its planned course, which would take it abreast of Narvik later that day. Fraser intended to sail that evening and to move Force 2 into a position where it could support the convoy if it were attacked. However, it was important to remain undetected, which meant trying to avoid enemy U-boats and reconnaissance air-craft until after the *Scharnhorst* had sailed.

By noon Fraser had some useful information. At 10:10 hours a Soviet reconnaissance plane – a lend-lease Spitfire – flew a photo-graphic reconnaissance mission over the Altenfjord. The pictures, taken at 8,000 feet, revealed the damaged *Tirpitz* at anchor at the head of the Kåfjord with a repair ship alongside her. In the Langefjord the *Scharnhorst* was still at anchor at its western end, while a group of three destroyers (Z29, Z34 and Z38) were anchored halfway between the battlecruiser and the eastern end, where it opened into the main Altenfjord. What the photo reconnaissance missed were the remaining two destroyers of the 4th Destroyer Flotilla – Z30 and Z33, which were anchored in a bay on the eastern side of the Kåfjord.

By lunchtime news of the sighting had been passed to Rear Admiral Burnett by the Russians, and within an hour the information was relayed to Admiral Fraser. It arrived at the same time as a top secret 'Ultra' decrypt from London – a German signal reporting the sighting of Convoy JW 55B by the Luftwaffe weather plane. Fraser was also warned of U-boat activity in the Barents Sea, south-east of Bear Island. This told Fraser that while the *Scharnhorst* had not yet put to sea, she would almost certainly make a sortie against the exposed convoy. It meant that he still had time to move his naval chess pieces exactly where he wanted them.

By then the Junkers 88 weather plane was not the only German aircraft to have spotted the convoy. At 11:25 hours another Junkers 88, flying from Bardufoss near Tromsø in northern Norway, spotted Convoy JW 55B some 400 miles west of Narvik, steering a course of 030° at a speed of 10 knots. It confirmed that, rather than containing forty troopships, the convoy consisted of just twenty merchantmen and twelve escorts. The position given was 67° 07′ north, 01° 45′ west, which placed the convoy to the west of Narvik. Then, at 12:30 hours, a second sighting report provided even more information. It claimed that the convoy consisted of seventeen merchantmen (each of 10,000 tons), and three tankers, deployed in seven columns, with the tankers in the centre of the convoy. The escorts consisted of three or possibly four cruisers, plus nine destroyers and corvettes. While this overestimated the strength of the convoy escort, it was a reasonably accurate estimation of the size and deployment of the convoy.

Then came another enigmatic report, passed to Admiral Bey's staff on board the *Tirpitz* by Kapitän-zur-See Peters, the captain in charge of U-boat operations in Norway. This time the sighting was made by a Blohm & Voss 138 flying boat, which was equipped with a rudimentary form of radar. It reported a sighting of one cruiser and five destroyers at 68.09° N. 00.01° E, which placed the force a little to the north-east of the convoy itself, and steering a course of 090°, as

Day 4: Thursday, 23 December 1943

if heading directly towards the Lofoten Islands, which covered the Vestfjord and the approaches to Narvik. The aircrew also reported a second force, some 9 miles to the north-west, this time of approximately twenty ships. The signal suggested this force might be a strong Battlegroup, operating at a distance from the convoy. More German reconnaissance planes scoured the area but no other sighting was made. In all likelihood the crew of the flying boat had spotted the convoy itself, and the force of warships was merely the ships of the Through Escort, rounding up the morning stragglers.

However, by noon it had become clear to Rear Admiral Boucher that his convoy had not only been spotted again but that German aircraft were taking turns to shadow it as he sailed north. At 11:40 hours lookouts on board HMS *Orwell* off the port side of the convoy spotted two Dornier 217 bombers approaching from the north-west. The aircraft sheered away, then took up position astern of the convoy, where the lookouts could hear the German planes but couldn't see them through the low cloud. These stalkers and their replacements continued to dog the convoy until nightfall. Occasionally they appeared through the low cloud, and both HMS *Haida* and HMS *Iroquois* fired on them but to no effect. The planes simply pulled back a little and disappeared into the safety of the clouds and general murk. Captain McCoy sent a signal to Admiral Fraser and Rear Admiral Burnett, informing them that Convoy JW 55B was being shadowed. Little did he know that this was exactly what Fraser had wanted. It looked like the Germans were about to take the bait.

In the Eyjafjördur Admiral Fraser read these reports, and surmised that Bey had to make his move within the next thirty-six hours or else risk the convoy eluding him. Force 2 had completed refuelling and taking on stores, so the admiral decided to let his men enjoy a few more hours of shore leave in Akureyri, then have his force set sail later that evening. The brief respite off the Icelandic port was certainly enjoyable – the locals spent the afternoon and early evening skating as far as the ice-bound battleship, while sailors enjoyed their few hours ashore buying whatever souvenirs – and alcohol – could be had in the small town. The admiral himself took an hour to stroll through the town, accompanied by Captain Russell of his staff. On his return to his flagship in mid afternoon it was already dark, and as he recalled in his diary, 'The Icelanders ashore were skating, by light – we were in darkness of course'. He decided to make the most of the picturesque moment: 'I asked the band to come up on deck and play Christmas carols; and really, it almost brought tears to your eyes.'

At 18:00 hours the admiral requested his captains and staff to meet on the flagship for drinks and a captains' conference. At 17:00 hours the meeting began in earnest as Fraser outlined his strategy for the coming battle, and then went on to discuss tactics. As he put it later, he wanted to make sure that 'every officer and man be doubly sure that he knew his night action duty. Such a reminder would hardly seem necessary, except that within the Home Fleet there are frequent changes of officers and men and, with constant escort requirements, adequate training is not easy to achieve.' He left nothing to chance when he described the coming battle. He planned to locate the enemy using radar and then to close within 12,000 yards before illuminating the *Scharnhorst* using star shells. Then the *Duke of York* and the *Jamaica* would use their fire control radars to pour shells into her. The *Jamaica* was ordered to stay in close support of the battleship, but he gave Captain Hughes-Hallett the freedom to take drastic action and open the range if he needed to: in other words, if the cruiser was pursued by the *Scharnhorst*. Fraser then told his destroyer captains that he planned to divide them into two groups, and then launch them in torpedo attacks designed to deliver the coup de grâce once the big guns had crippled the enemy battlecruiser.

Fraser realised that his big tactical advantage was radar. The *Duke of York* carried twelve different radar sets, of four types. Her main surface search radar was the Type 273 Q, which had an effective range of 23 nautical miles. In addition her type 281 air search radar had an air warning range of 100 miles but also worked as a back-up surface search radar, with a range comparable to the Type 273 Q. Finally, she carried several fire control radars, designed to direct gun-fire against a target. The Type 284 radar served her main armament and had a range of 24 nautical miles. It could therefore provide radar control for her 14-inch guns at their extreme range of 38,000 yards. A similar system (Type 282) provided guidance for the battleship's anti-aircraft guns. In late 1943 this suite of electronics made the *Duke of York* one of the most sophisticated radar platforms in the Royal Navy. The *Jamaica* had a similar suite of radars, although she was fitted with a slightly older and less reliable version of the Type 273 set.

Day 4: Thursday, 23 December 1943

By contrast the *Scharnhorst* had a radar range of just 8 miles, and relied on optical guidance for her main guns.

The captains' conference wound down around 19:00 hours, and as it closed, the admiral issued sailing orders for 22:00 hours. Meanwhile, the one senior member of the admiral's staff who didn't attend the conference was Lt. Cdr. 'Dickie' Courage, the fleet signals officer. That evening he conducted his own exercise – a communications test between the ships of Force 2, designed to test the group's ability to coordinate movements by radio during a night surface action. Each ship had its own call sign and code book, and Courage wanted to make sure that all the signallers in the force knew what to expect when the action started. As he put it: 'I felt it important that the signal ratings should be familiar with the race card before the actual race took place.'

Of course there was a risk involved – the signals could be intercepted by German listening stations, but Courage later said that 'the risk had been considered and accepted' – it was 'probably no more than the possibility of police radios in the countryside of Sussex being heard in Glasgow'. As events would show, while the Germans didn't detect these signals, their listening stations did manage to pick up radio chatter the following day, which confirmed Admiral Bey's suspicions that Convoy JW 55B had a covering force. The signal exercise concluded with the *Duke of York* sending the signal: 'Make to Admiralty – *Scharnhorst* sunk.' As Courage put it, 'I was somehow certain we should be making that signal in due course.'

At 22:00 hours the *Duke of York* sheeted home her anchor and turned away from the lights of Akureyri, heading north into the darkness of the Eyjafjördur. A small group of minesweepers of the 1st Minesweeping Squadron led the way up the long fjord, followed by four destroyers – HMS *Savage* and HMS *Samaurez* of the 1st Sub Division, HMS *Scorpion*, and the Norwegian destroyer HMNoS *Stord* (formerly HMS *Success*) of the 2nd Sub Division. All four were 'S&T' class destroyers. The small ships were followed by the *Duke of York*, while the *Jamaica* brought up the rear. It was pitch black and the lookouts couldn't see the mountains on either side of the fjord as their ships steamed north towards the open sea. It was also bitterly cold, and reports suggested the weather would deteriorate over the next few days.

The Battle of North Cape

Out in the Norwegian Sea Convoy JW 55B ploughed on through the darkness, which gave her a temporary respite from the shadowing aircraft of the Luftwaffe. Rain and sleet showers battered the ships as they sailed north, while the weather forecast for the next few days promised much worse to come. A severe gale was expected to hit the Barents Sea by Christmas morning and already the rough seas and strong southwesterly winds – already approaching gale force – made conditions extremely uncomfortable, if not dangerous. Many of the merchant ships were having problems maintaining their position, and the speed of the convoy was frequently being reduced to allow stragglers to catch up. The convoy was dangerously exposed to enemy attack – but then, that was exactly what the British had intended.

The ships of Convoy RA 55A enjoyed better weather – the worst of the building storm front lay ahead of them. By nightfall on 23 December the convoy was well out into the Barents Sea, having spent the day heading north, to give the Germans in the Altenfjord as wide a berth as possible. The empty merchant ships were now heading west, skirting close to the southern edge of the polar icecap. The plan called for the convoy passing close to Bear Island during the early hours of Christmas morning, then to continue westwards until the convoy passed the longitude of Jan Mayen Island (07° W), which would bring it safely out of range of German aircraft.

The warships of Rear Admiral Burnett's Force 1 sailed from the Kola Inlet that morning, and they shadowed the convoy northwards for 200 miles, before altering course westward early in the evening of 23 December. That meant that all four of the Allied formations were at sea, approaching the battleground off North Cape from two different directions. Meanwhile, although the situation may have looked reasonably straightforward on the charts in Admiral Fraser's cabin, the worsening weather meant all his carefully laid plans might be put in jeopardy. The biggest variable was the *Scharnhorst* itself. Fraser had already stationed a submarine – HMS *Sirdar* – at the entrance to the Altenfjord, with orders to report if the battlecruiser put to sea. Fraser could be reasonably confident he would know when the Germans made their move. Beyond that he could only hope that everything went according to plan and that, in the darkness of the Arctic winter, he would be able to find the enemy before the *Scharnhorst* found the convoy.

Day 5: Christmas Eve – Friday, 24 December 1943

Those who were at sea that morning don't really remember a dawn, just a faint lightening of the blackness. Three days after the shortest day of the year the sun never appeared over the horizon, even if the lookouts could see through the sleet and snow squalls and low, scudding black clouds. In these conditions the term 'daybreak' was only relative, as the best that could be hoped for was a few hours of twilight around the middle of the day. Worse, the weather had deteriorated during the night and the southwesterly gale was building in intensity, and moving steadily towards the Barents Sea. These were hardly the most favourable conditions in which to fight a battle, but there was little choice. In fact both sides hoped to use these conditions to their advantage: the Germans, by approaching Convoy JW 55B without being detected; and the British, by hiding the two covering forces until the *Scharnhorst* came within range of their guns.

At 07:00 hours Rear Admiral Boucher gave the order that would set Convoy JW 55B onto a new course – 057° – which would bring it around the top of the Norwegian coast, heading for Bear Island and the edge of the ice shelf. It also committed the convoy to the passage through the Barents Sea, and to running the gauntlet of the Altenfjord. Like most convoys, course changes were made in increments, to avoid unnecessary confusion amongst the merchant ships, whose captains were unused to manoeuvring in concert. However, this particular convoy seemed much worse than most. At dawn several of its ships had become stragglers and, as they did every morning, the escorts began rounding up the wayward merchantmen and ushering them back into position. This thankless task was made particularly hazardous as the rough seas were becoming so mountainous that it became extremely dangerous to move within hailing distance of another ship.

The most persistent offender was the *Ocean Gypsy*, a 7,000-ton Empire Liberty Ship built in Portland, Maine, but now operated on behalf of the Ministry of War Transport by the British shipping company J&C Harrison's of London. She was supposed to be the rearmost ship of Column 5, but almost every morning she was found well behind the rest of the convoy. The escort commander, Captain McCoy, even quipped that 'All that can be said is *concordant nomine facta* (our deeds agree with our name)'. He added that, collectively,

The Battle of North Cape

the merchant ships of Convoy JW 55B 'had shown that it was incapable of reasonable station-keeping'. Another troublemaker was the American Liberty Ship *Thomas V. Walter*, whose crew seemed incapable of working the radio or signalling their intentions. As McCoy put it: 'Even the simplest Morse signal took 30 minutes to pass to her. One message was broadcast on R/T six times, but she did not receive it.' This made any course change a frustrating and occasionally dangerous exercise – in rough seas and poor visibility the risks and problems were greatly increased.

While Boucher was doing his utmost to keep his convoy on track, Admiral Fraser was reading a sheaf of fresh signals. One report, gleaned from 'Ultra', revealed what the German reconnaissance reports had contained the previous day. First was the report by the Junkers 88 reconnaissance plane during the forenoon, which mentioned twenty merchantmen and twelve escorts, and gave the course and speed of Convoy JW 55B as 030° and 10 knots respectively. Fraser also saw the second, more detailed, report, issued shortly after noon, which spoke of seventeen merchant ships and three tankers, in seven columns. Finally, there was the mystery report of a cruiser and five destroyers to the east of the convoy, which was clearly an erroneous sighting. It was this last signal that worried Fraser the most. If the Germans suspected the convoy was being protected at a distance by one or more covering forces, then there was a possibility Admiral Bey might decide not to send his Battlegroup to sea.

That morning the admiral's flagship was involved in a last-minute exercise, along with the rest of Force 2 and its destroyer entourage. *Jamaica*, accompanied by the destroyers *Savage* and *Samaurez*, played the part of the *Scharnhorst* and two German escorts, moving south-west of the main force until they reached a bearing of 150° from the destroyers *Scorpion* and *Stord*, who played the part of convoy escorts. They were supposed to be guarding an imaginary convoy on a course of 060°, maintaining a speed of 12 knots. The *Duke of York* played herself, shadowing the convoy from a distance and waiting for the 'enemy' to make her move.

The aim was for the *Duke of York* to fire her 14-inch guns at the *Jamaica*, but to aim short, so the salvos fell a safe 4,000 yards in front of the 'enemy battlecruiser'. When this happened the *Jamaica* was allowed to take evasive action – something she would do in real life

Day 5: Christmas Eve – Friday, 24 December 1943

if the *Scharnhorst* fired at her – steering within 30° of her agreed northerly course. She was even allowed to return fire, aiming her salvos so they were 'thrown off', landing 4,000 yards astern of the *Duke of York*. In terms of a radar and navigational exercise everything worked smoothly, and both the battleship and the cruiser managed to track their opponents on radar. However, at the last minute the shoot itself was cancelled – the seas were considered too rough for a live firing exercise – after all, a slight roll of the ship at the wrong moment could easily send the shells 4,000 yards over or to the right, which meant they could land on their friendly adversary. Both Captain Russell of the *Duke of York* and Captain Hughes-Hallett of the *Jamaica* declared themselves pleased with the way their gunnery teams performed. Everyone knew the next time the crews would go through the same motions it would be in earnest – and the enemy would be firing back.

At noon, Convoy JW 55B was approximately 360 miles to the north-west and making slow progress. As it was designated a 'fast convoy', JW 55B was expected to maintain a steady speed of 10 knots. So far it had managed to hold its speed fairly well, but by the morning of Christmas Eve a combination of bad weather and indifferent seamanship on the part of the merchant captains had managed to slow the force down. That morning it had only managed to make an average speed of 8½ knots, and at 11:30 hours Boucher ordered the convoy to reduce its speed even further to just 7 knots, to allow stragglers to catch up. Not only had some ships managed to become detached during the night, but others found it all but impossible to make the course change expected of them earlier that morning, and consequently the convoy had begun to straggle again. Boucher and McCoy were well aware that convoy discipline was all-important, as JW 55B was now less than 400 miles from the Altenfjord – well within range of a surprise attack by the German Battlegroup.

To make matters worse, the Luftwaffe had returned, despite the atrocious flying conditions and poor visibility. At 12:25 hours HMS *Iroquois* spotted two aircraft shadowing the convoy from astern, and the same aircraft were later spotted by the escorts protecting the port side of the convoy. The two visitors were Junkers 88 bombers, flying a reconnaissance mission from Bardufoss airfield, midway between Narvik and Tromsø. At 12:20 hours one of these two aircraft sent a signal back to its base, reporting that the convoy was now at 70° 27'

47

north, 03° 35′ east, and steering a course of 050° at a speed of 8 knots. This was pretty accurate information – the noon position recorded by the flag navigating officer on board the *Fort Kullyspell* was 70° 40′ north, 03° 10′ east – just 13 nautical miles from the position plotted by the Luftwaffe. This meant that the Germans now knew exactly where the convoy was, and given its limited options once it passed between Bear Island and North Cape, they could predict its future course with a fair degree of accuracy.

The position of the convoy was also worrying Admiral Fraser. On board the *Duke of York* he and his staff plotted the location of Convoy JW 55B and his doubts about the efficacy of using it as bait began to re-emerge. Effectively, he wanted the convoy to pass close enough to the Altenfjord to tempt the *Scharnhorst* into sailing, but not close enough that it couldn't escape if needed to. He recorded his thoughts in his diary: 'Although German surface forces had never before made a sortie to the westward, the convoy which had now reached a position 70° 40 N 03° 10 E at 12:00 was entirely unsupported, and I was uneasy lest a surface attack should be made.' It was a fine line, and after re-examining the positions of the two convoys and the two naval forces in relation to the Altenfjord, he decided that the line had been crossed. He had deliberately put Convoy JW 55B in harm's way and there was now a serious possibility that the *Scharnhorst* could attack before either of the two naval groups could come to the rescue.

Consequently, at noon, Fraser ordered the breaking of radio silence and sent a signal to Rear Admiral Glennie – Commander of the Home Fleet Destroyer Flotillas, based on board the depot ship HMS *Tyne*, in Scapa Flow – requesting the transfer of four fleet destroyers from the 'D3' (the Fighting Destroyer Escort of Convoy RA 55A) to D17 (Captain McCoy's escort for JW 55B) 'should the opportunity arise'. He also suggested that Convoy RA 55B should maintain a more northerly course than planned after passing Bear Island, just in case it ran into the *Scharnhorst* without its full complement of destroyer escorts. Copies of the signal were sent to the commanders of both convoys and convoy escorts, to Rear Admiral Burnett in Force 1, and to the Admiralty. The convoys should pass within 200 miles of each other within the next twenty-four hours, which meant that the destroyer reinforcements could probably reach Convoy JW 55B before Force 1 could reach the area. It was a sensible precaution – and a

Day 5: Christmas Eve – Friday, 24 December 1943

'request' from the Commander-in-Chief of the Home Fleet was simply a direct order, wrapped up in gentlemanly courtesy. An hour and a half later Fraser broke radio silence again, this time to send a signal directly to Captain 'Bes' McCoy in HMS *Onslow*, who was the escort commander of Convoy JW 55B. This time the request – to be relayed to Rear Admiral Boucher – was to: 'Reverse your course until 17:00 hours.' At the same time he ordered Force 2 to increase speed to 19 knots. He explained the reasoning behind these two orders in his diary: 'If the enemy surface forces had searched to the westward, this step would have had little effect in bringing the convoy closer, but it would have prevented the convoy being located by them before dark.' In other words, this served a two-fold purpose. Fraser couldn't guarantee that the *Scharnhorst* had not already put to sea that afternoon without him knowing about it. It kept Convoy JW 55B more than 400 nautical miles from the Altenfjord until the twilight of daytime turned to the pitch black of night. Even if the *Scharnhorst* had sailed the previous evening, she would be incapable of managing more than 20 knots in these conditions, and therefore it made sense to keep the convoy out of range as a precaution. Second, it slowed the convoy's forward progress, which gave Force 2 a better chance of working into a position between the convoy and the Altenfjord by the end of Christmas Day.

The only problem was that Rear Admiral Boucher knew full well it was an order that was impossible to follow. Less than six and a half hours ago he had altered the course of his convoy by 30° and it took the best part of two hours to sort out the mess to his neat convoy formation made by merchant captains who seemed unable – or even reluctant – to follow naval orders. Ships had veered off course, columns had become intermingled, and stragglers had to be rounded up. If that level of chaos resulted from an incremental change of course of just 30°, then two successive course alterations of 180° were completely impossible. He and his flag navigating officer pored over the chart and made some hurried calculations.

After conferring with Captain McCoy, Boucher reached a compromise. It was now a little after 14:00 hours. In a perfect world, with biddable and conscientious merchant skippers, if the order to reverse course was given within the hour – say at 15:00 hours – it would take approximately half an hour to turn the convoy around. The same would happen at 17:00 hours, which meant it would be back on its original position by 19:00 hours. If it then continued at 10 knots for twelve hours until 07:00 hours, it would have advanced 120 nautical miles from its present position. It could achieve the same purpose another way, without any manoeuvring. It was decided that the convoy would stay on its present course but would reduce speed to 8 knots until the following morning. It was a pragmatic and straightforward solution to an impossible problem. Certainly, it increased the risk of a daylight encounter with the *Scharnhorst*, if she was at sea, but this risk was considered acceptable compared with the horrors involved in turning the convoy.

More significant than this flurry of orders from the flagship was the fact that they had been made at all. Admiral Fraser's decision to break radio silence was a calculated risk. It might reveal the presence of the covering force – the one thing he didn't want to happen. However, the risk was probably justifiable. He knew Convoy JW 55B was dangerously exposed. It had already been spotted by German reconnaissance aircraft, and the enemy only had a limited window of opportunity to launch an attack against it. In order to do so success-fully, the German Battlegroup needed to be at sea already or make a sortie before nightfall the following day. The convoy had effectively played her part, and by ensuring it was better positioned and pro-tected, Fraser was greatly reducing the risk to his bait. Fraser himself addressed the problem in his diary: 'The RA Convoy had obviously remained undetected. This inclines me all the more to the opinion that our own convoy will be attacked. The U-boats are almost certainly already on its trail. The *Scharnhorst* will come out and attack this convoy. I am more than ever convinced of this.'

The non position report of Convoy RA 55A placed it close to Bear Island, which meant it had completed the most dangerous portion of its voyage, and with every passing hour it now moved further away from the Altenfjord. The admiral's instructions to continue west before turning south towards the British Isles further guaranteed its safety. This meant that his decision to reallocate the bulk of its destroyer escort to the more vulnerable JA 55B convoy was fully justified.

Another factor was that Fraser was conducting a naval campaign in almost impossible weather conditions, involving forces operating

Day 5: Christmas Eve – Friday, 24 December 1943

hundreds of miles apart. It involved detailed calculations regarding course, speed, fuel reserves, firepower, weather and visibility. For example, the destroyers accompanying Force 2 had barely enough fuel to remain in the operational area for two days. That meant that Fraser's decision to sail from Iceland on the evening of 23 December was based on his best estimate of when the Germans would pose the greatest threat to his convoys. It was inevitable he would have to issue orders to all these units during the course of the operation, as he needed to be able to fine-tune his plans, and to counter any moves made by his German opponent. If this meant occasionally breaking radio silence then the risks this involved were considered acceptable, weighed against the need to coordinate his forces. He would do the same thing several times throughout the next three days, particularly during 26 December, when his warships were moving in for the kill.

The problem with the early afternoon signals sent on Christmas Eve was that they *were* detected by the Germans – an intelligence break-through that could have cost Fraser the success he craved. At 18:30 hours Generaladmiral Schniewind in Kiel was passed a message from the intelligence gathering section at German Naval Headquarters. It reported that a radio signal had been detected by two Radio Direction Finding stations, one at Kirkenes in northern Norway, the other near Cuxhaven on the German North Sea coast. The disquieting news was that, by plotting the relative bearings of the signal from both stations, it appeared that the signal originated from somewhere in the Barents Sea, approximately 180 miles astern of the last plotted position for Convoy JW 55B. Schniewind wrote: 'The British unit whose bearings have now been acquired at an extremely acute angle, appears to be approximately 180 nautical miles astern of the convoy. This may be an approaching covering force. We must take into account the presence of a second enemy force in the Barents Sea, unless it is thought the fix is so unreliable that it emanates from the convoy itself, or from a straggler. There is nothing revelatory about this fix.' The German Admiral's worst fears were justified. The radio message that had been intercepted came from Admiral Fraser's flagship. What is so surprising is the way Schniewind seems to have convinced himself the fix was unreliable. If the presence of a covering force was suspected, then the sensible course would be to cancel any sortie by the *Scharnhorst* until the report could be investigated. But that would compromise the

The Battle of North Cape

success of the operation, depriving the Kriegsmarine of the face-saving operation it so desperately needed.

Of course, the Germans had other sources of intelligence. The Luftwaffe had been ordered to look out for any group of ships operating within striking distance of the convoy, but so far no other ships had been detected. Kapitän-zur-See Peters, commanding the U-boat force in Norway, was probably not surprised. On the day Convoy JW 55B sailed from Loch Ewe he wrote to Schniewind: 'It must be recorded that the Luftwaffe's reluctance and lack of strength in the north mean that there is no chance of a successful attack by the U-boats and the Battlegroup.' This was a pretty bleak assessment of the abilities of the Luftwaffe in Norway, but it was aimed more at shifting potential blame than anything else. Peters continued: 'It is essential that Fleet Command make this unequivocally clear, so that the Navy is not blamed for the fact that supplies to Russia are passing through the Barents Sea without loss.'

Even the U-boat commander must have admitted that, over the past few days, the Luftwaffe had done well to locate and then shadow Convoy JW 55B. Peters even said as much to Admiral Bey that morning, even before the reconnaissance aircraft had re-established contact with the convoy. In a message to Bey he stated that, in his opinion, the Luftwaffe had made an adequate job of shadowing the convoy. He also suggested extending the search area 300 miles to the west, just in case a covering force was lurking somewhere beneath the storm front. When Peters learned of the radio direction fix he felt his worries were justified. This coincided with the news that three of the four Blohm & Voss 138 flying boats fitted with radar had been grounded that day, two with technical problems and the third due to the weather. That meant that the chances of locating a covering force in the Barents Sea were greatly reduced. Peters realised that, without adequate aerial reconnaissance, it was up to his U-boats to act as the eyes and ears of the Kriegsmarine.

That evening Peters had eight U-boats under his command. The U-boats of the Eisenbart group were strung out in a long screen at right angles to the likely path of an enemy convoy, with its centre about 130 nautical miles south-west of Bear Island. Only seven boats were in the screen – *U-277* had just spent forty days on patrol in the Barents Sea, her crew was exhausted, and she was running short of fuel. That evening she was heading back to Narvik, where she would be refuelled and sent straight back out to sea. In Narvik, Peters could do little other than wait for his U-boats to sight the convoy, although that evening he did order the screen to be contracted, concentrating his boats closer to the likely point where the convoy would cross the screen.

U-601 was in the centre of the line, and her inexperienced commander, Oberleutnant-zur-See Hansen and his crew were celebrating Christmas Eve, 40 metres beneath the storm-tossed surface of the Barents Sea. An officer described the celebratory dinner that evening:

> On each plate is a packet of biscuits, a bar of chocolate, a box of pralines, a piece of marzipan, apples and bon-bons ... A long, white-draped table has been laid in the crews' quarters in the bow. Our sailors' Christmas tree, made of scraps of green-painted metal and rope ends, looms large at the head of the table ... All lights have been switched off. Just one, in a Christmas-like lampshade at the end of the table is left on. Our Captain says a few well-intentioned words about the meaning of the Christmas festival, and why we have to celebrate it up here in the far north, far away from home.

The celebrations were over by 22:00 hours, at which point Hansen took his boat to the surface to send a radio report, and where he received fresh orders from the U-boat base in Narvik. Despite being buffeted by waves that dwarfed the small U-boat, *U-601* turned south and slowly made her way towards her newly-assigned position, based on Kapitän-zur-See Peters' latest intelligence about the course and speed of the convoy. While only one or two boats could reach the area by the following morning, at least Peters was doing what he could to make a contact between the two groups a little more likely.

Peters and his U-boat crews knew that reconnaissance reports had placed Convoy JW 55B to the south-east, and it was expected that the Allied ships would reach the line of waiting U-boats some time on Christmas morning. In the convoy itself the escort commander, Captain McCoy, had been told of intercepted radio signals, suggesting that a group of U-boats lay somewhere ahead of him. However, the seas were too rough to make a successful torpedo attack likely, while he had faith that the captains of his escort vessels were professional enough to deal with any threat posed by the enemy.

By December 1943 the German U-boat fleet was fighting at a disadvantage. Most Allied escorts now carried powerful radar sets, capable of locating a U-boat on the surface long before the German lookouts could see the enemy. Radio triangulation equipment (known as 'Huff-Duff'), the use of airborne centimetric radar by Allied sea-planes, and the success of Operation Ultra – the breaking of German naval signals codes – all meant that the Allies tended to know where U-boats were expected to operate, and could therefore route their convoys accordingly. Worse, latest developments in sonar technology meant that it was now much easier for escorts to detect the presence of a U-boat, and either to avoid the threat or to launch an attack against the submersible. In effect, U-boats were no longer the hunters – they could also be hunted – and convoys with a substantial escort screen were now extremely difficult to penetrate. That evening, Peters and his commanders were well aware that the odds were stacked against them.

Day 6: Christmas Day – Saturday 25 December 1943

The full force of the southwesterly gale was felt in the Barents Sea during the early hours of Christmas morning. Two Allied convoys were being subjected to its wrath: Convoy RA 55A, heading westward towards Greenland; and a little to the south-west, Convoy JW 55B, heading deeper into the Barents Sea. Early that morning Admiral Fraser (whose Force 2 was some 60 miles astern of this second convoy) had decided the two convoys would not pass each other close to Bear Island as anticipated, for the progress of JW 55B had been slower than expected. He had already altered its course further to the north, in an attempt to maintain its distance from the Altenfjord, while at 02:00 the 36th Destroyer Division (HMS *Musketeer*, HMS *Matchless*, HMS *Opportune* and HMS *Virago*) had detached themselves from RA 55A, and headed south, aiming to achieve a rendezvous with Convoy JW 55B later that day. The two forces were now approximately 100 miles apart, and the destroyers had to sail directly into the oncoming gale.

Day 6: Christmas Day – Saturday 25 December 1943

Oberleutnant-zur-See Hansen recalled the effect the Force 8 gale had on *U-601*:

> It is pitch-dark. Look out! cries the Officer of the Watch. The boat heels severely – we cling on for all we are worth. A wave breaks over us, cold sea water falls over our faces and shoulders, taking away our breath before pouring into the conning tower. We are surrounded by a sea whose ferocity is beautiful to witness. The boat cuts its way through a series of waves whose crests tower eight or ten metres above us ... From our conning-tower it is an awesome sight ... rolling black mountains of glistening water ... ragged clouds scud across the sky. In the few seconds available to us we scan the horizon through our binoculars. We are here to search for enemy ships ... again the bow plunges deep into a wave. The next wave is a big one, its crest edged in white. It breaks against the conning-tower with a crash like that of a freight train crossing a railway bridge. The spray lashes our faces – it is as though someone has thrown a handful of grit at us.

Shortly before 09:00 hours, Hansen had enough of this battering and gave the order to dive to 60 metres – a depth that would protect the boat from the storm and give his men the opportunity to listen out for approaching enemy ships. But the boat had barely submerged when the sonar operator reported the sound of a vessel approaching from the south-west. That was the most likely direction the enemy convoy would appear from. Soon other contacts were heard, and it became evident that the convoy was on course to pass directly overhead. Hansen steadied his depth at 40 metres and waited. It took twenty minutes for the convoy to pass, and inside the U-boat the sound of its engines and propellers would have been deafening.

Hansen waited another twenty minutes before giving the order to surface – he had to make sure he didn't appear directly in front of some tail-end escort. *U-601* broke the surface at 09:50 hours, and two minutes later a signal was sent to the U-boat base in Narvik, reading: 'Run over by Convoy in Square AB6720. Enemy steering 60°. Hansen.' Convoy JW 55B had been spotted. Less than thirty minutes later the signal had been deciphered by the naval signals staff in Narvik, and a copy was handed to Hansen's superior, Kapitän-zur-See Peters. This was exactly what he wanted to hear. He recorded in his diary that 'the position of the convoy was established as planned'. Within an hour the same signal was placed on the desk of the Fleet Commander in Kiel, Generaladmiral Schniewind.

Like Peters, Schniewind had already established to his satisfaction that the ships which had passed over *U-601* belonged to an Arctic convoy. The night before, German naval analysts had reported to him that 'Course, speed and composition make it possible to say with certainty that this is a PQ Convoy bound for Murmansk or the White Sea.' Schniewind added: 'I share this view. Such questions as still remain open may be expected to be answered when the convoy passes the U-boat cordon tomorrow morning.' Oberleutnant-zur-See Hansen's sighting report had simply confirmed what everyone already knew.

Of course, the job of the U-boat men was far from over. Hansen had been in exactly the right place, but other boats were converging on the likely position of the convoy. The next boat in the screen, to the south of Hansen, was *U-716*, commanded by Oberleutnant-zur-See Dunkelberg. The boat had only just arrived in Arctic waters and Dunkelberg was eager to see action. He set a course towards the north-east, running with the gale, and after five hours of misery he and his lookouts were rewarded with a glimpse of an escort destroyer. It was just before 13:00 hours. The destroyer was soon hidden by the wind and rain but the sonar operator reported it was a steady contact, at a range of 3,000 metres. Dunkelberg promptly fired an acoustic homing torpedo down the bearing, but it soon became clear that he had missed, and the sound of the contact disappeared towards the north-east.

Approximately a mile away on Dunkelberg's port side, Hansen had regained contact with the convoy. Having sent his signal he gave chase, but progress was hampered by the gale, which seemed to be getting stronger. At 11:02 hours he sent another signal to Narvik: 'A destroyer and a number of shapes 90 degrees true.' A little after noon he followed this with another signal: 'More merchantmen and a large destroyer with two funnels.' His surface shadowing of the convoy was a dangerous undertaking – at any moment he could be detected by enemy radar, and a group of destroyers could be vectored in on his position, depth charges at the ready. Then, at the same moment as

Day 6: Christmas Day – Saturday 25 December 1943

Dunkelberg was waiting for his torpedo to hit, Hansen spotted a British destroyer dead ahead of him, and less than 500 metres away. He immediately dived the boat and stayed at 40 metres for another thirty minutes. By the time he surfaced again the destroyer had gone – but so had the convoy.

Some distance to the north-west another U-boat was trying to approach the convoy. *U-636*, commanded by Kapitänleutnant Hildebrand, was to the north of *U-601* when it intercepted Hansen's first message, and Hildebrand set a course to intercept. However, this put his boat at right angles to the direction of the gale, and a particularly big wave broke over the conning tower, sending tons of icy water crashing through its open hatch into the boat itself. The water flooded the engine room, stopping one of the engines, and landed up in the battery compartment, where the water caused a reaction, producing clouds of chlorine gas. *U-636* was now without power, beam on sea, and filling up with poisonous gas. His engineers finally managed to restart the engine, and the boat turned into the wind, away from the convoy. At 14:50 hours Hildebrand sent a signal to Narvik: 'Because of the presence of a lot of Chlorine Gas am only just able to dive. Am breaking off to Hammerfest.'

Hildebrand aired the boat on the surface as best he could, then, around 18:00 hours, the damaged *U-636* dived again. As he submerged, Hildebrand heard the sound of approaching ships, and soon the convoy passed overhead. He stayed submerged for another four hours, until, at 22:00 hours, he surfaced to air the boat. He finally reported the sighting to Narvik: 'At 18:00–19:20 in AB6496 run over by eight cargo vessels and three escorts. Easterly course, 70 RPM. No contact. Poor listening conditions, visibility 800 metres.' However, by that time, Kapitän-zur-See Peters had a pretty sound appreciation of the convoy's course and speed and felt confident that men like Hansen and Dunkelberg could track the convoy until the *Scharnhorst* could intercept it.

While Hildebrand was heading for the nearest port, Hansen was still chasing after the convoy. He had another close call at 16:36 hours, when *U-601* was almost run down by a corvette, which suddenly appeared through the murk less than 300 metres away. For the second time that afternoon Hansen crash-dived the boat, but it soon became apparent that the lookouts on the escort hadn't spotted them. That was the last U-boat contact of the day. Despite the appalling flying conditions the Luftwaffe was managing to fly a few of its missions, and at 11:15 hours a Dornier 217 located the convoy. However, the increasing ferocity of the storm kept its colleagues on the ground and contact was eventually lost. That meant it was up to Peters and his U-boats. Effectively, Convoy JW 55B had managed to pass through the U-boat screen without incident, and was now working its way towards Bear Island, its progress covered by the gale.

At least the Germans knew where the convoy was, and what course it was steering. Both the U-boats and the Luftwaffe had completely failed to detect Convoy RA 55A, while both Force 1 and Force 2 were approaching the waters off the North Cape and the Altenfjord, and so far the Germans might have suspected their presence, but had no hard information to back these suspicions up. The day before, Generaladmiral Schniewind had dismissed the reports which suggested a covering force might be lurking behind the convoy. He knew the Kriegsmarine needed a victory, ostensibly to help relieve the pressure on the Russian front, but more accurately to help restore the damaged credibility of the German surface fleet. That meant bold action – taking a risk. The problem was that as commander of the Battlegroup, Konter-Admiral Bey was far from resolute, and it seemed as if Bey was grasping at any opportunity to avoid having to lead a winter sortie.

At 02:30 hours on Christmas Eve morning, Admiral Bey sent a pessimistic signal to Kapitän-zur-See Peters, which began by commenting on the likelihood of a covering force. He stressed that: 'A search for enemy covering forces is essential', which showed he didn't share Schniewind's optimism. He then went on to discuss the limited tactical options available to him if the Battlegroup sailed:

> The best time for tactical surprise would not be early dawn, measured astronomically, but at half-light in the middle of the day ... At a probably northern meeting point there will be no light at all, which means that conditions will not be at all conducive to the employment of heavy guns.

More than thirty-six hours later the tactical problems facing the *Scharnhorst* still existed, and if anything the deteriorating weather

Day 6: Christmas Day – Saturday 25 December 1943

made the effectiveness of Bey's destroyers even more of a problem than before. Worse, there was still no sign of any covering force.

The following day Peters replied, saying that:

> If the Battlegroup putting to sea does not become known to the enemy and tactical surprise is achieved, an engagement of two to three hours' duration may be counted on, and nine to ten hours allowed for withdrawal.

He added that he felt it unlikely that any British naval group could overtake the German Battlegroup during this withdrawal, and suggested that a naval engagement could be fought at ranges of up to 17,700 metres despite the poor light levels. Whether Peters believed all this is less important than his realisation that the Admiral needed all the encouragement he could get. That evening, Generaladmiral Schniewind added his own comments, agreeing in principle with Bey, but striving to boost his confidence. He added that:

> the situation calls more for action by destroyers than by the entire Battlegroup, unless an especially favourable situation in the battle area materialises, accompanied by good visibility, possibly in the shape of the Northern Lights, good weather, and a clear picture of the enemy's dispositions.

On Christmas Day there was precious little sign of either visibility or good weather. Strangely enough, Schniewind finished up by stating that, while he recommended leading an attack with the destroyers, he had his reservations about their effectiveness. He wrote:

> Guidelines have therefore been drawn up for deploying the destroyers primarily in the winter. Because of their lack of strength, conditions do not really favour them.

In effect, he sounded almost as pessimistic as Admiral Bey.

However, by the evening of Christmas Eve, Schniewind had already made up his mind. By the following morning the convoy would be less than sixteen hours' steaming from the Altenfjord. He realised that the

The Battle of North Cape

Kriegsmarine's window of opportunity was closing. As he wrote these comments his headquarters staff were already drawing up the draft orders for a sortie by the Battlegroup. At 23:37 hours that night the draft was sent to Grossadmiral Karl Dönitz for approval. As the Commander-in-Chief of the Kriegsmarine, Dönitz had the final say in the deployment of any of the remaining capital ships of the fleet. On Christmas Eve he was in Paris, attending a dinner held in honour of his leading French-based U-boat commanders. Observers recall he was unusually taciturn during the dinner, as if he had a lot on his mind. Dönitz knew what was coming and was busy weighing up the options.

On Christmas morning Dönitz was handed a copy of the draft order. He took the document with him when he boarded his private transport plane, which flew him back to his headquarters outside Berlin. By the time the plane landed, Dönitz had read the draft orders and had written his comments. At 14:12 hours his staff called the office of Generaladmiral Schniewind in Kiel, informing him of the Grossadmiral's approval of the plan. Within the hour this was followed up by a written teleprinter message: 'The Battlegroup will sortie in time to allow it to operate against the convoy.' The die was now cast. For his part, Schniewind had now waited for almost fourteen hours for a reply from his superior, and so he wasted little time in passing on the order. Shortly after 14:30 hours the message 'Ostfront 25/12' was sent to the office of Kapitän-zur-See Peters in Narvik, with orders to forward it to Admiral Bey on board the *Tirpitz*.

Peters was enjoying a Christmas lunch on board the *Grille*, the floating headquarters of the Kriegsmarine in Norwegian waters. Although sometimes referred to as Hitler's yacht, the handsomely appointed *Grille* was actually a fully operational warship, having been used as a minelayer before her conversion into a headquarters ship. Peters immediately ordered the signal to be repeated to Admiral Bey, and within half an hour the decrypted signal was being handed to Admiral Bey. He ordered it to be redirected to Kapitän-zur-See Hintze on board the *Scharnhorst* and to Kapitän-zur-See Johannesson on Z-29. However, this time Bey added one important addition. This time it read: 'Ostfront 1700/25/12' – the *Scharnhorst* was now due to set sail at 17:00 hours. Bey also gave orders for the transfer of him and his staff from the battleship to the battlecruiser.

Day 6: Christmas Day – Saturday 25 December 1943

On board the *Scharnhorst* the crew were already cursing the admiral for spoiling their Christmas. Shortly before 11:00 hours that morning Bey had ordered the battlecruiser to go to one hour readiness for sea at 13:00 hours. Many of the crew thought this was nothing less than a ploy by the Kriegsmarine to dampen the festivities. Until then the Christmas celebrations had been in full swing – Kapitän Hintze had conducted his Christmas rounds of the ship, distributing cigarettes, and the latest mail had been delivered, which for many included parcels from home. The ship's choir was singing Christmas carols over the ship's loudspeaker system, and all were at peace with the world. If the first signal spoiled this tranquil picture of a Christmas in port, the second message ruined Christmas completely. Norwegians living on the shores of the Altenfjord remember seeing Christmas trees washed up on the shore the next day, as the sailors threw their decorations overboard. The 'Ostfront' message had upset a hornet's nest, as the officers and men raced to prepare their ship for departure.

Earlier that morning a signal had been sent to the minesweeper *R-122*, ordering it to deliver three local pilots from Tromsø to the Battlegroup. One was assigned to the *Scharnhorst*, the others to the destroyers *Z-29* and *Z-33*. The minesweepers *R-56* and *R-58* were ordered south from Hammerfest, with orders to report to the captain of the *Scharnhorst* on their arrival. Their job would be to escort the Battlegroup through the German minefields that protected the entrance to the Langefjord. They arrived shortly after the 'Ostfront' message was received. The minesweeper captains, Maclot and Hauss were small-boat sailors, and the battlecruiser represented a different kind of naval world:

> We are led through a confusing maze of passageways, watertight doors, companionways, cabins, workshops, telephones, cables, pipes, power decks and mess decks.

By the time they reached the captain's day cabin they would have been hopelessly lost. There they were issued their instructions, and Hintze handed Maclot a last letter to post to his wife, as the mail-boat had already left. The pair were dismissed, then escorted through the ship to meet the signals officer, who discussed communications protocols before sending them on their way.

The Battle of North Cape

Maclot later recalled that 'there is feverish activity everywhere ... the ship is like an anthill that has been disturbed.' They were relieved to return to their own small 'Räumboote', which were tied alongside the battlecruiser. There they waited. The scheduled departure time passed, and still the orders to cast off never came. The delay was caused by Admiral Bey, whose departure from the *Tirpitz* had been delayed. At 14:00 hours he and his 36-man battle staff had transferred to the destroyer *Z-30*, but she still had to embark her own supplies from the supply ship *Nordmark* before she could put to sea. Therefore it was 18:30 hours when Bey was finally piped on board the *Scharnhorst* – ninety minutes after her scheduled departure time. Finally, at 19:00 hours, Hintze gave the order to weigh anchor. And so the *Scharnhorst* began her last voyage.

Two tugs were on hand to guide the battlecruiser down the Langefjord, while *R-56* and *R-58* duly took station as ordered, astern of the flagship. As the *Scharnhorst* weighed anchor a launch delivered written orders to Johannesson on board *Z-29*. Another destroyer, *Z-38*, preceded the battlecruiser down the fjord, where it would rendezvous with *Z-29* and the rest of the Destroyer Flotilla once the battlecruiser passed into the wider channel of the Altenfjord. As soon as the *Scharnhorst* was under way Hintze ordered all spare crew to muster on the afterdeck, where they were addressed by the First Officer, Fregattenkapitän-zur-See Ernst-Dietrich Dominik. His morale-building talk was simple and straightforward: 'A convoy is on its way with supplies for the Eastern Front – our task is to annihilate that convoy.' The crew were then dismissed.

Shortly after 20:30 hours the *Scharnhorst* passed the anti submarine boom that marked the entrance to the Langefjord, and after picking up a shore party who met her there, she turned north towards the open sea. Once in the more open water of the Stjernsund, the *Scharnhorst* picked up speed and ordered Johannesson's destroyers to make 17 knots. Unfortunately, the accompanying minesweepers could only manage 16 knots and were slowly left behind. The Battlegroup would have to find its own way through the gap in the minefield – a potentially dangerous situation that was probably a calculated risk on the part of Admiral Bey. He realised he could afford no further delays, so he decided to rely on the skills of his navigators rather than the minesweepers to reach open water.

Day 6: Christmas Day – Saturday 25 December 1943

At 21:10 hours the speed was increased to 25 knots, and once through the narrow Stjernsund, the admiral ordered *Z-29* and two other destroyers to form a 'V-shaped' anti-submarine screen ahead of the flagship. The remaining two destroyers fell in astern. Just after 23:00 hours the Battlegroup passed Point Lucie, the navigational beacon that marked both the entrance to the Altenfjord and the end of the defensive minefield. The ships were now well enough away from the protective cover of the land to feel the full force of the gale, which by now had swung round so that it blew from the south-south-west. It was particularly tough for the 'class 1936A' destroyers, which all carried twin 5.9-inch guns in their forward turrets, a modification that increased their firepower at the expense of drastically decreasing the vessels' sea-keeping qualities. It would be an extremely uncomfortable night for Johannesson and his destroyer crews. Once he was safely past Point Lucie, Bey ordered a course change to 010°, and so the *Scharnhorst* and her escorts began the long journey north towards Convoy JW 55B. Operation 'Ostfront' had begun.

His target – Rear Admiral Boucher's convoy – lay approximately 250 miles to the north-west. If the Battlegroup could maintain its course and speed, then it would reach Convoy JW 55B around 11:00 hours the following day – the hour Bey had already described as perfect for fighting a gunnery action using visual rangefinders in the Arctic twilight. In the convoy itself, Christmas Day had been something of an anti-climax, despite having to negotiate the Barents Sea in the midst of a Force 8 gale. At 7:43 hours Captain McCoy sent a gloomy situation report to Boucher on board the *Fort Kullyspell*:

> Situation today. Enemy will probably attack us today with U-boats and possibly surface craft. Four more Home Fleet destroyers should join us p.m. today. *Duke of York* is about 100 miles astern, coming up at 19 knots or more. Three heavy cruisers are somewhere ahead. Happy Christmas.

With the exception of the one torpedo fired by *U-716* at 13:00 hours, the U-boat attacks never materialised, and the convoy passed through the U-boat screen without incident. A few contacts were detected, and at one stage depth charges were dropped on a possible U-boat, but otherwise progress had been uneventful. At 12:50 hours the destroyers *Matchless*, *Musketeer*, *Opportune* and *Virago* joined the convoy from the north, and within an hour had taken up station on its starboard flank – between the convoy and the Altenfjord. Two of McCoy's destroyers and a corvette then detected another U-boat contact some distance to port, and spent a fruitless hour trying to locate the enemy boat. In all probability this was Hansen's *U-601*, which almost ran into a corvette at 16:36 hours, but this was the last U-boat contact of the day. The convoy continued on its way into the Arctic night.

News that these four extra destroyers had reached the convoy was passed to Admiral Fraser that afternoon, who now 'felt confident that if the *Scharnhorst* attacked the convoy, Force 1 and the escort destroyers would either drive her off or inflict damage which would give me time to close.' Meanwhile, the *Duke of York* and the rest of Force 2 steamed on in pursuit of the convoy at a slightly reduced speed of 17 knots. After all, as Fraser put it with as much reserve as he could muster: 'There was an unpleasant sea.'

All the forces were now at sea – Convoy RA 55A was now out of the danger area, but Convoy JW 55B was still in danger, and the German Battlegroup was heading northwards on a course to intercept her. So too was Force 1, currently 200 miles from her and to the east of Bear Island, while Force 2 was 100 miles astern and closing fast. Apart from the westbound convoy, all these forces were heading through the darkness towards the same small area of ocean, some 180 nautical miles beyond North Cape, or 240 nautical miles from the mouth of the Altenfjord.

Day 7: Sunday 26 December 1943

The Middle and Morning Watches (00:00–07:59 hours)
When the German Battlegroup turned north at Point Lucie it experienced the full force of the storm. In fact the destroyers had already found it tough going as they emerged from the narrow Stjernsund into the more open waters at the head of the Altenfjord. The problem lay in their design. These *Zerstörer* ('destroyers') Type 1936A were often referred to as the 'Narvik' class, largely because many of them formed the 8th 'Narvik' Destroyer Flotilla, which had operated together in Norwegian waters since late 1940. The basic design was sound

Day 7: Sunday 26 December 1943

enough – these vessels were just under 400 feet long with a 40-foot beam and a displacement of around 3,600 tons. The destroyers had a clipper bow and high forecastle, which stepped down abreast of the bridge to form a continuous after deck. They had been laid down before the war, and Z-29 and Z-30 were launched in late 1940 – in time to replace the Kriegsmarine's heavy destroyer losses in the Norwegian campaign earlier that year. The idea was that their design incorporated many of the lessons learned during the first year of the naval war.

This, of course, was not strictly true. The Type 1936A destroyers were a little larger than those of the Type 1936 they replaced, mainly because they were designed to carry a heavier armament. While the earlier destroyers carried five 127mm (5-inch) guns in single turrets, the Type 1936A ships were designed to carry five 150mm guns (6-inch), one in a twin turret in the bow, and the remainder in single mounts towards the stern. However, production problems meant that the C-38 twin turret wasn't available when the destroyers were being fitted out, so a single 150mm gun was mounted in the 'A' turret position as a stopgap. While the twin turret was eventually fitted to Z-29, Z-30 still carried a single gun in her forward turret when she sailed out of the Altenfjord.

The three other destroyers – Z-33, Z-34 and Z-38 – were all built during the war, and formed a sub-class known as the Type 1936A (Mob). These were virtually identical to the earlier group of destroyers, distinguishable mainly by a different type of curved cap over the forward funnel. They all carried the twin 150mm turret forward, just like Z-29. The real problem with the 'Narvik' class design lay with this forward turret. First of all, experience showed that the gun was harder to operate than its smaller 127mm predecessor, as it needed separate shells and powder charges. The older destroyers used single composite shells. As the single turrets were open to the elements, this made the guns difficult to operate in Arctic waters.

Even more seriously, the turret arrangement was top-heavy, adding 97 tons to the weight of each destroyer, and seriously reducing the seakeeping qualities of the vessels. In effect, the extra weight made them bad sea boats, the weight preventing the forecastle from riding the waves well, and therefore making the vessels plough into on-coming waves rather than break through or over them. Consequently,

The Battle of North Cape

they shipped a lot of water over the bows, and in anything other than calm seas the forecastle was awash with sea water. The extra weight also made these destroyers roll heavily in rough seas. While this was bad enough in ordinary conditions, these problems were magnified considerably when the ships went to sea in an Arctic gale.

In fact, Kapitän-zur-See Peters in Narvik had already expressed his concern for their safety, in a signal sent to the German Naval Headquarters in Kiel, written as the German Battlegroup was heading for the open sea. First, at 20:00 hours, he put a telephone call through to Admiral Schniewind. Peters expressed his concern about the weather: 'The destroyers have no chance in this weather.' He added that the Luftwaffe reported that there would be no improvement the following day (26 December), and that the Battlegroup would find it virtually impossible to locate and engage the enemy convoy in these conditions. He finished the call by recommending that the operation be cancelled. Forty minutes later Schniewind sent an urgent message to Grossadmiral Dönitz at his headquarters outside Berlin. In effect it supported Peters: 'Conditions are very unfavourable. Significant results cannot be expected. Therefore propose cancellation.' As the *Scharnhorst* entered the open waters of the Barents Sea the fate of the operation now rested with Dönitz. Would he accept that the operation should be cancelled, or would he put operational considerations behind the need of the Kriegsmarine to show it was playing its full part in the war?

The reasoning behind Peters' dramatic request was given in his diary for the previous evening, which read:

No one knows where the enemy covering force is, if it even exists. The weather has deteriorated faster than has been predicted, with the result that both the speed and the firepower of the German ships will be severely curtailed. The U-boats are unable to keep up with the convoy, so it will not be possible to direct the Battlegroup to the target. The element of surprise will have been lost. Instead it must be assumed that the *Scharnhorst* and her escorting destroyers will find themselves fighting the enemy's superior covering force, instead of the convoy's weaker escort force.

This was an extremely pessimistic interpretation of events, albeit a logical one.

Day 7: Sunday 26 December 1943

At 21:15 hours Admiral Bey broke radio silence to send a situation report to Kiel: 'In the Area of Operations a 6–9 South-Westerly is forecast. The destroyers' ability to bring their armament to bear greatly hampered. Speed reduced.' That was before the Battlegroup had even reached the open sea. It was clear that Bey was having second thoughts, and the weather provided him with an excellent reason to cancel the operation. While he was unable to do so himself, Bey evidently expected either Schniewind or Dönitz to see reason. However, Bey's signal never reached Dönitz until early the following morning – around 04:00 hours. By that time Dönitz had already made his feelings clear. Regardless of the appalling weather conditions the operation would go ahead as planned. Whether he might have acquiesced after reading Bey's signal is a matter of conjecture. That evening all the Grossadmiral could base his decision on was the latest sighting reports from aircraft and U-boats, the latest radio direction-finding reports, and the recommendations of both Peters and Schniewind. The reply from Grossadmiral Dönitz was handed to Bey a little after midnight. It read:

Important enemy convoy carrying supplies and munitions to the Russians further imperils the heroic struggle of our army on the Eastern front. We must help.

Attack the convoy with the *Scharnhorst* and destroyers.

Exploit the tactical situation with skill and boldness. Do not break off the battle with the task incomplete. Go all out and see the mission through. Your greatest advantage lies in the superior firepower of the *Scharnhorst*. Her contribution is therefore vital. Deploy the destroyers as you see fit.

Disengage if you judge that the situation demands it. Break off automatically if heavy forces are met with.

Inform the crews accordingly. I have every confidence in you.

Heil und Sieg, Dönitz, Grossadmiral.

That left Bey with no more room for manoeuvre. Operation Ostfront would go ahead as planned. His only leeway was that the destroyers could be detached if Bey thought it necessary.

Two other messages were delivered at the same time. One informed Bey that the U-boats of Gruppe Eisenbart were ordered to sweep the likely path of the convoy at dawn until contact was regained. The other was from the Luftwaffe, reporting the sighting contacts of the previous day (25 December). It claimed that aircraft had shadowed the convoy for four hours (12:25 until 16:25 hours), and so its course and speed were known. Even more importantly, the Luftwaffe report added that there was no sign of a covering force within 50 nautical miles of the convoy. At least he now had a reasonable idea of where his target was, and what to expect when he attacked it. The only trouble was that these Luftwaffe reports were the best part of eight hours old. There was no guarantee the convoy would maintain its course and speed throughout the night.

As the Battlegroup headed north, Bey would have worked out the geometry of the problem facing him. Given the information provided by U-boats and aircraft, the likely position of the enemy convoy at dawn was approximately 240 nautical miles due north of Point Lucie – the entrance to the Altenfjord. If the Battlegroup could maintain its present speed of around 25 knots, and its course of 010°, then the *Scharnhorst* and her destroyers could expect to make contact with the enemy some time around 09:30 hours the following morning. Of course, all this depended on the convoy doing exactly what was expected of it, and the top-heavy German destroyers being able to cope with the mountainous seas.

As the Battlegroup crashed onwards towards the north, Bey signalled his Destroyer Flotilla Commander, Kapitän-zur-See Johannesson on board Z-29. According to Johannesson, it was around 03:00 hours when Bey asked his opinion on the weather. By that time the Battle-group was now 100 miles north of Point Lucie and about 50 miles past the tip of North Cape. That meant that the *Scharnhorst* and her labouring destroyers were now approaching the epicentre of the storm, which meteorologists had placed about 50 miles north of North Cape at midnight. The destroyer commander signalled back: 'With sea and wind from astern we have had no difficulties so far. I expect the weather to improve.' As Johannesson put it afterwards: 'I was not willing to provide Bey with an excuse to send us back to base, as long as the British destroyers were coping with the weather.'

While Johannesson had chosen to sound optimistic, many of his men would have relished the opportunity to turn back to port. After all, many of them were inexperienced sailors, and the weather conditions were testing the endurance of these raw seamen to their limits. The top-heavy destroyers would have been rolling dangerously, even though – as Johannesson pointed out – they were now running with the gale, rather than pushing against it. The lookouts could barely make out the other ships of the Battlegroup in the darkness, while the ice-cold wind and the freezing spray would have made conditions on deck almost unbearable. Those below decks were protected from the weather, but still had to put up with the violent rolling and cork-screw motion of the destroyers through the water, and the nagging fear that they were sailing into the teeth of a gale in ships that were poorly designed for these conditions.

Around the same time – 03:00 hours – a second signal was handed to Bey, this time from the German Naval Headquarters in Kiel. It was the reply to the message Bey had sent almost six hours before, when he first became worried about the weather. It said:

> If destroyers cannot keep sea, possibility of *Scharnhorst* completing task alone using mercantile warfare tactics should be considered. Decision rests with admiral commanding.

Although this was no last-minute cancellation of the operation, at least it gave Bey the flexibility he needed to go it alone if the weather deteriorated. However, this coincided with Johannesson's optimistic signal implying that the destroyers were coping perfectly well. The result was that Bey decided to keep the destroyers with the Battlegroup.

At 04:00 hours the Middle Watch came to an end, and while one group of sailors returned to their messdecks another watch reported for duty. Kapitän-zur-See Hintze used this opportunity to make an announcement, passing on the contents of the signal from the Grossadmiral. Seaman Günther Sträter, manning one of the port side 5.9-inch guns on board the battlecruiser, remembered the announcement:

> Captain to all Stations. A wireless message has been received from the Grossadmiral: Seize the convoy whenever and wherever you get the chance – you will be relieving pressure on the Eastern Front. Signed, Dönitz, Grossadmiral.

The Battle of North Cape

The message was met with enthusiasm. Despite the weather, the crew of the *Scharnhorst* were eager to play their part.

Bey's confidence was also boosted when he was told of an intercepted radio message, sent from Oberleutnant-zur-See Dunkelberg in *U-716* to the U-boat base at Narvik. It had been intercepted by *Z-29* at 03:30 hours and was duly passed on to Bey. It stated: 'Square AB6642. forced to dive by escort. South 7, Sea 6–7, Visibility 1,500 metres.' Johannesson recorded the signal in his diary, adding:

> According to this the enemy is about 30 nautical miles further west than assumed. This is good news for us. The convoy's course is confirmed. Because we are delayed this is very welcome news.

Both Bey and Johannesson believed they were still very much on course to intercept the convoy. However, some 250 miles to the southwest of the German Battlegroup another admiral was about to alter the delicate geometrical balance between hunter and prey.

At 02:16 hours Admiral Fraser on board the *Duke of York* was handed an 'Ultra' signal, sent from the Admiralty in London. It read: 'Emergency. *Scharnhorst* probably sailed 6pm, 25 December.' Fraser now knew that the enemy was at sea. A second 'Ultra' signal sent immediately after the first reported that the *Scharnhorst* had signalled that it expected to be passing the boom protecting the Langefjord at 18:00 hours. The problem with 'Ultra' was that British Naval Intelligence knew they had to be sparing with the information they issued, for fear the Germans would discover that their naval codes had been broken. Fortunately, they also had supporting evidence from another source – Norwegian intelligence gatherers. That meant that, at 03:19, the Admiralty could confidently send out a second signal, issued to all Allied warships in Convoy JW 55B, Force 1 and Force 2. It read: 'Admiralty appreciated that *Scharnhorst* is at sea.' This second message was effectively a cover signal, designed to disguise the fact that 'Ultra' intelligence had already informed Admirals Fraser and Burnett that the enemy was at sea.

Armed with this information, Fraser would have consulted his chart. He knew it would have taken the *Scharnhorst* and her escorts the best part of five or six hours to reach Point Lucie from the Langefjord boom, which meant that she would have begun her northwards run to

Day 7: Sunday 26 December 1943

intercept the convoy at around midnight. He knew that Bey's window of opportunity – when there was sufficient daylight to engage the convoy using visual targeting – was limited to a few hours on either side of noon. He also realised that the convoy had been shadowed, and was probably still being followed by enemy U-boats. That meant that Admiral Bey knew where it was. It was a simple matter of mathematics to work out that the *Scharnhorst* would need to maintain a speed of around 25 knots during her run northwards, which meant that Fraser could predict with some degree of confidence where he expected the German Battlegroup to be at dawn the following day. In other words, Bey's actions were predictable. Fraser now had to make sure his own actions were not.

The situation at around 04:00 hours showed that contact was likely to take place within about five hours. First, Convoy JW 55B was rolling uneasily through the heavy seas, some 50 nautical miles south of Bear Island. She was making a speed through the water of approximately 6–8 knots, and maintaining a course of 060° (east-north-east), although the sea conditions made it hard to maintain any semblance of formation. Rear Admiral Boucher and Captain McCoy planned to continue towards the north-east until the convoy reached the southern edge of the ice pack, and then to follow the edge of the ice to the south-east until it reached the longitude of Murmansk. Then the convoy would head southwards towards the safety of the Kola Inlet. That way the convoy would keep as much distance as it could between it and the *Scharnhorst*. Convoy RA 55A was well clear of the danger area, and at 04:00 hours it was 220 miles due west of Bear Island, maintaining a westerly course. Despite the bad weather the convoy would make good time, and would arrive at Loch Ewe without incident on 1 January.

Rear Admiral Burnett's Force 1 was 150 miles east of Convoy JW 55B, and 145 miles east-south-east of Bear Island. The force was heading on a course of 235° (west-south-west) at 18 knots, the maximum speed Burnett's cruisers could manage while sailing into the gale. His plan was that by 10:00 hours he would reach a position approximately 30 miles due east of the convoy, and would therefore be in a position to support it if it were attacked. In effect, the convoy and Force 1 were on reciprocal courses, with the naval force a little to the south of the convoy. This meant that Burnett was not only well-placed to protect it, but that he should intercept the *Scharnhorst*

The Battle of North Cape

before the German battlecruiser could reach the convoy. Finally, there was Force 2, which was 210 miles to the south-east of the convoy, steering a course of 084° (east). Although Fraser's force was making 24 knots, the destroyers were finding progress extremely heavy going, and even the battleship itself was experiencing problems in the rough seas.

Just after 04:00 hours Admiral Fraser broke radio silence again, as he sought to reposition his forces. He had already ordered the ships of Force 2 to prepare to increase speed, in case the *Scharnhorst* decided to cut back towards the Altenfjord. He then ordered Convoy JW 55B to alter course to the north, and to continue on a northerly heading until the *Scharnhorst* was located. In fact, Rear Admiral Boucher decided to delay the course change for an hour or so until the light improved, and it was after 06:00 hours before the convoy finally turned away from the likely track of the *Scharnhorst*. Fraser and Burnett exchanged details of position, course and speed, and as a result the admiral decided to move his pieces again.

At 06:30 hours Fraser ordered the convoy to move onto a new heading of 045°, which would move it closer to Force 1, and at the same time he ordered Burnett to close with the convoy and support it. Of course, Burnett was effectively doing this already, but by changing the course of the convoy Fraser realised that Burnett needed to alter course slightly to compensate. Fraser also ordered Burnett to increase speed to 25 knots – a speed that was only just possible, given that he was now heading broadside onto the gale, rather than directly into it. Burnett altered course to the west, planning to work his way round to intercept the convoy from the east-south-east. That way he would reduce the effects of the gale as much as possible, while keeping his force between the convoy and the enemy.

The last element in the great geometrical puzzle was the German Battlegroup. At 04:23 hours Bey ordered his ships to alter course to port, onto a new heading of 030°. Presumably this was an attempt to move the force a little to the east, in case the convoy managed to slip past the Battlegroup in the post-dawn twilight. However, less than forty minutes later, at 05:00 hours, he resumed a more northerly course of 003°. An hour later the crews were called to breakfast and at 07:00 hours Kapitän-zur-See Hintze ordered the *Scharnhorst* to go to action stations. Since the days of fighting sail this was a standard

Day 7: Sunday 26 December 1943

precaution for warships sailing in dangerous waters as dawn came up. Hintze was taking no chances. After all, the convoy – or worse, a hitherto undiscovered covering force – could be just a few miles away in the darkness.

At 07:00 hours Bey ordered the Battlegroup to deploy into scouting formation, where the destroyers were deployed ahead of the battlecruiser. However, to provide the earliest possible warning to the *Scharnhorst*, Bey ordered his destroyers to take up position 10 nautical miles ahead of the battlecruiser. That placed them well beyond visual range. All communications would therefore have to be by radio rather than by visual signals. Bey also reduced the speed of the Battlegroup to 12 knots. Finally, he ordered the Battlegroup to alter course by 130° to port, onto a new heading of 230°. Given the intelligence at his disposal, this seems a strange manoeuvre. After all, the sighting by *U-716* had placed the enemy convoy to the north-west, not the south-west. It is possible that Bey had forgotten the time delay involved in transmitting, receiving and decoding signals, or that U-boats often repeated their signals until receipt was acknowledged. He may well have placed the convoy further to the south-west than it actually was.

For Bey, the whole operation was dogged by poor, delayed or even non-existent communications. By 07:00 hours the convoy was a dozen miles further north than the position given by *U-716* would have supposed, and would still have been even if Fraser had not ordered JW 55B to change course. If Bey had remained on course he would probably have intercepted the convoy a little after 09:00 hours. After all, at 07:00 hours it was little more than 30 miles away to the north-west. Instead he lost time and latitude as his Battlegroup scouted towards the south-west. These two decisions – to place the destroyers beyond visual range, and to alter course to the south-west – were to play an important part in what was to follow. In the short term they would deny Bey the opportunity to fall upon the convoy, and ultimately they would rob him of the chance of success in the coming battle.

The Forenoon Watch (08:00–11:59 hours)

Nobody who survived the destruction of his command knows what made Konter-Admiral Bey give the order. In any event, it robbed him of his last chance of success in the battle to come. At 08:00 hours, his German Battlegroup was heading towards the south-west, with the five destroyers of the 4th Destroyer Flotilla deployed in line abreast, some 10 miles ahead of the *Scharnhorst*. The whole formation was steering 230° at a speed of 12 knots, and its target – Convoy JW 55B – was less than 30 miles away. In all likelihood the northernmost of the destroyers would cross the path of the convoy some time before 10:30 hours. Bey's plan seemed to be working. Then, just twenty minutes later at 08:20 hours, Bey gave the order that turned the *Scharnhorst* round to the north. For some reason the course change was never passed to Kapitän-zur-See Johannesson in *Z-29*, whose destroyer lay in the centre of the screen. The *Scharnhorst* was now heading away from Johannesson at an obtuse angle of 130°. Every ten minutes that passed placed the *Scharnhorst* and her escorts 4 miles further apart. The result was that these destroyers would play no further part in the battle that followed.

The reason for the change of course may have been a routine signal from Oberleutnant-zur-See Hansen in *U-601*, which the *Scharnhorst* picked up at 08:14 hours. Bey might have assumed the signal marked the location of the convoy, and set off on a course to intercept. Alternatively, the battlecruiser might have detected something on its Seetakt radar, which the operators thought might be a part of the convoy. However, later events suggested it was unlikely that the radar was switched on, for fear of being detected by Allied detection equipment. We will never know. Unknown to the German admiral, this new course placed him in between the convoy and Rear Admiral Burnett's Force 1, which was approaching from the east-south-east. Burnett was further to the south-east than he had hoped to be, and consequently, at 08:00 hours, he was still 50 miles away from the convoy. However, he was also heading directly towards the *Scharnhorst*.

Johannesson was having his own problems. By 09:00 hours the *Scharnhorst* was about 24 miles away to the north-east, but the destroyer commander believed she was still somewhere behind him. Shortly afterwards the lookouts on board *Z-29* spotted the dark shape of a destroyer to the north-north-west. The next destroyer in the line was the *Z-30*, and her lookouts spotted the ship too. Johannesson sent a signal to Bey, informing him of a sighting, but minutes later the destroyer turned out to be one of his own – *Z-38*. She should have

Day 7: Sunday 26 December 1943

been on the far right of the flotilla line, but for some reason she had strayed off course and was now cutting ahead of the other two vessels. Unknown to everyone involved, if *Z-38* had stayed on course it might well have come across the rear of the convoy. As the flotilla commander signalled her to return to position the lookouts spotted something else through the murk – a pale glow away to the north-east. It was 09:26 hours.

What observers in the 4th Destroyer Flotilla perceived as a pinkish glow was actually a star shell, and it had just burst directly over the *Scharnhorst*, bathing her in light. The Germans were taken completely by surprise. Everyone who saw it must have froze for a second or two, as the Arctic night turned so unexpectedly into day. Seconds before, Bey must have felt himself completely in control of the situation, about to fall upon a completely unsuspecting enemy convoy. Suddenly he had become the prey.

In fact, the star shell had been fired by Rear Admiral Burnett's flagship HMS *Belfast*, which was 13,000 yards away to the south-east. The British had been following the *Scharnhorst* for the best part of an hour. At 08:34 hours a 'jig' – an unidentified radar contact – had been picked up on the Type 273 surface search radar on board HMS *Norfolk*. At the time Force 1 had been steering a course of 305° at a speed of 8 knots. The contact was at a bearing of 280° – to the west – at a range of 33,000 yards (16½ nautical miles). The report sent alarm bells ringing throughout the three British cruisers – this was exactly why they had battled their way through an Arctic gale. However, Burnett was alarmed by its position, as it meant that if the contact was the *Scharnhorst*, then she was less than an hour's steaming away from the convoy. Six minutes later the contact was detected by the *Belfast*, and ten minutes later, at 08:50 hours, HMS *Sheffield* acquired the same target. All three British cruisers were now tracking the contact, and the gunners were working out fire control solutions to help direct shells directly onto the hidden target. From its course and speed there was no doubt that it was the *Scharnhorst*.

Actually, a combination of 'Ultra' intelligence reports and signal direction finding meant that both Admiral Fraser and Rear Admiral Burnett had a pretty good idea where the *Scharnhorst* should be that morning, and the contact was roughly in the right place. For Burnett his mission was clear: he had to protect the convoy. As he put it afterwards:

> The part that our cruisers had to play in this action was, from my point of view a fairly simple one. I dare to say that I had certain experience in these waters. I knew exactly what our Commander-in-Chief wished us to do. I was completely confident that the captains serving under me knew what was in my mind, and would carry on as I wished them.

About 30 miles away to the west-north-west Captain McCoy knew that his convoy escorts might have to fight to protect their charges. Therefore he concentrated his destroyers on the threatened side of the convoy. The four vessels of the 36th Destroyer Division still formed their own distinct unit, under the command of Commander Fisher in HMS *Musketeer*. McCoy ordered Fisher to form a screen some 6 miles to the south-south-west of the convoy – a form of early warning against any attack by the German battlecruiser and her destroyers. At that point the convoy itself was heading due north at 8 knots. Like Johannesson, McCoy spotted the flares to the east-south-east at 09:26 hours, which told him that the *Scharnhorst* was over in that direction, and that Force 1 had found her. Unlike his German counterpart, he would have found the pink glow reassuring.

At 08:00 Force 1 had been steering a course of 235° at a speed of 8 knots. However, fifteen minutes later McCoy sent Burnett the latest estimated position of Convoy JW 55B, along with her course and speed. As a result, Burnett turned his force to the north-east, and minutes later *Norfolk* reported her 'jig'. By glancing at the tactical plot, Burnett could see that the convoy lay on an approximate bearing of 287°, which meant the *Scharnhorst* was not only closer to the convoy than Force 1 was, but that it seemed to be between his cruisers and the convoy he had been ordered to protect. However, by the time the *Sheffield* acquired the 'jig' at 08:50 hours it had become clear that instead of steaming towards the convoy, the contact was actually now steaming heading south, away from it.

At 09:00 hours Burnett ordered his three Cruisers to form on a bearing of 180° from the flagship, on a course of 325°. This effectively placed his ships in a staggered line, like a one-armed 'V' formation,

Day 7: Sunday 26 December 1943

where the *Sheffield* and then the *Norfolk* were echeloned to port of the *Belfast*. This meant that all three ships could fire forward or directly to port without the other cruisers obstructing their line of fire. However, the effectiveness of the formation relied on the enemy contact remaining within the firing arc of the guns. If it moved too far to the north or to the south-east the fire of two of the ships could be masked. By that time the 'jig' was approximately 18,000 yards away, or 9 nautical miles.

To confuse matters further, *Belfast* then picked up a second 'jig' to the north-west, on a bearing of 299°, at a range of 24,500 yards (12 nautical miles). That meant she was now tracking one large contact to the south-west and another smaller one to the north-west, both roughly at the same range. In all likelihood this was HMS *Virago*, the destroyer on the right of Commander Fisher's convoy screen – the one sent out as an early warning picket by Captain McCoy. For a few anxious minutes Burnett and his staff considered the possibility that she was a German destroyer – the eastern end of a line of enemy warships. It soon became evident that she matched the course and speed of the convoy, as reported by McCoy less than an hour before. This made it unlikely the mystery contact was a German warship and Burnett gave orders to disregard the contact.

By this time all three cruisers were at action stations, and their guns were ready and manned. All three cruisers had radar-guided fire control systems, which meant that the course, speed and bearing of the enemy 'jig' were being analysed and updated all the time. This same information was being passed to observers on the gunnery direction platforms, where gunnery staff used optical rangefinders to follow the enemy. That way the spotters knew in which direction to look. In late 1943 visual gunnery direction was still more accurate than radar-guided gunnery, but the new radar technology was reliable enough to use effectively when visibility was poor. That morning the visibility was not just poor, it was atrocious. Even with night-sighting equipment the British lookouts were barely able to see more than 5 or 6 miles through the snow squalls. A seaman on the *Belfast* remembered the moment when the crews stood to their guns, having spent the night at their stations:

Everyone gets up, deflates and puts on their lifebelts which they have been using as pillows, the shellroom's crew start unshipping the bars which hold the shells in place in the trays. The magazine and handling room men go down to their respective stations and the hatches are closed on top of them. Everyone is tensed for us to open fire.

The range closed. At 09:15 hours the contact was 13,000 yards from the *Belfast* (6½ nautical miles) on a bearing of 250° – west-south-west. Burnett ordered the *Norfolk* and *Sheffield* to move round onto a bearing of 160° from the *Belfast*, in an attempt to provide the ships with a better angle of fire. In effect, he was making the angle of his formation a little more acute, thereby making the single-sided 'V' formation a little narrower. However, Force 1 still stuck to the same course – 325°. Then, at 09:21 hours, lookouts on board the *Sheffield* spotted a dark shape on the port beam. The time-honoured naval signal went out: 'Enemy in Sight', followed by details: 'Bearing 222°, Range 13,000 yards.' Burnett gave the order to Captain Parham of the *Belfast* to fire a 4-inch star shell along the bearing. That was the star shell that lit up the *Scharnhorst* – the opening shot of the Battle of North Cape.

The *Norfolk* opened fire with her 8-inch guns as soon as the star shell illuminated the target. Recovering from his surprise, Kapitän-zur-See Hintze ordered the *Scharnhorst* to turn 30° to port, onto a new course of 150°. As a result the *Norfolk*'s first salvo fell 500 yards away from the battlecruiser. To imagine the situation, think of a standard geometry set square. Before the course change, the *Scharnhorst* was heading down towards the right angled-corner, while Force 1 was steaming up the longest edge – the hypotenuse. The change of course by the *Scharnhorst* at approximately 09:28 hours now changed the geometry, putting her and Force 1 on what were almost parallel but reciprocal courses.

This was rapidly putting the battlecruiser out of the arc of fire of the two British light cruisers, whose fire was about to be obstructed by the *Norfolk*. Worse still, the 8-inch guns on the heavy cruiser still used non-flashless cordite, so the blast from them temporarily blinded the observers on the other two British ships. At first Burnett told the heavy cruiser to 'drop back, clear my range', but two minutes later, at 09:30 hours, he ordered the formation to turn 60° to port onto a new heading of 265°. By this time the guns of the two light cruisers

Day 7: Sunday 26 December 1943

were completely obscured and it would take time to make the change of course that would allow them to open fire. However, this course change did little to alter the overall geometry of the situation. The only difference was that the triangular set square had been tilted a little. The *Scharnhorst* was still sailing down one side towards the right angle, while Force 1 was steaming up the hypotenuse. Worse still, the *Scharnhorst* was steadily opening the range.

The good news for Burnett was that although the tactical situation was getting worse by the minute, the strategic situation was improving. Force 1 had now worked itself between the *Scharnhorst* and the convoy, which meant that he had managed his primary task of protecting JW 55B from attack. Therefore, at 09:38 hours, Burnett ordered another, even more dramatic, change of course, this time onto a new heading of 105°. While his previous manoeuvres had been designed to drive off the *Scharnhorst*, now he was actually giving chase. Still, the course change involved a turn of 160° – an almost complete reversal of course. This was a slightly more complicated manoeuvre than the previous turn, and more time-consuming. All this time the *Scharnhorst* was drawing further away.

Still, the *Norfolk* was scoring hits. She fired six salvos in just under ten minutes: the first at 09:29 and her last at 09:38. Watching from the *Belfast*, Commander Welby-Everard of Burnett's staff was 'fairly certain *Norfolk* got a hit with her third salvo, as I saw a flash as I watched her salvo fall.' As Captain Bain of the *Norfolk* put it: 'We were the first to sight the enemy. We were the first to open fire, and we were the first to score a hit.' However, the range was opening: by the time the *Norfolk* ceased firing at 09:40 hours the *Scharnhorst* was a full 24,000 yards away (12 nautical miles).

On board the *Belfast* and *Sheffield* the crews must have wondered why their main guns had still not opened fire. Captain Parham of the *Belfast* soon answered the question by making an announcement over the ship's tannoy: 'After a few broadsides from the *Norfolk* the enemy, whoever she may be, has turned away and we are now chasing her.' The same gunner who described going to action stations wrote:

This is a sign for everyone to relax and ask each other: 'Well, I wonder what she is. I hope we aren't up against the *Scharnhorst*.'

The Battle of North Cape

To all but a few lucky spotters and plotters, the 'jig' remained little more than an unseen mystery contact.

As well as altering course, Hintze had also ordered the laying of a smoke screen to confuse the British gunnery observers, and he had also rung for full speed. The *Scharnhorst* was now making 24 knots through the water, while the British ships had only increased their speed to 16 knots – the fastest they could manage in the gale force seas. When it came to speed through the water and the stability of a hull as a gunnery platform, larger ships have an edge over smaller ones, particularly in stormy conditions. Within just fifteen minutes of being surprised by the star shell, she had moved out to the extreme range band of the *Norfolk*'s 8-inch guns, reducing the chances of a hit in such poor weather conditions until they were almost negligible. On paper the extreme range of a British Mk VIII 8-inch gun was just over 30,000 yards (15 nautical miles). In practice it was much less, particularly when using radar fire control. Even the latest version of the Type 273 radar could only detect large contacts up to 18 nautical miles away – 23 miles under perfect conditions. That morning conditions were far from perfect. The range of effective radar gunnery fire control was approximately halved, which meant that, by 08:45 hours at the latest, the *Scharnhorst* was out of range.

It was at that point that Burnett decided to break off the action. As he saw it, his primary duty was to protect the convoy, not to pursue the *Scharnhorst*. This was an extremely difficult decision to make – Burnett was known as a fighting admiral rather than a thinking one, so it probably went against his instincts to break contact. However, the *Scharnhorst* was fast moving out of contact, and if he pursued to the south-east he would be drawn further away from the convoy. He still had no idea where the German destroyers were. Therefore, at 10:00 hours, he decided to move back towards the convoy, ordering a turn away from the enemy towards the north-west, onto a new course of 305°. This was another almost complete reversal of his present course. Fifteen minutes later he altered course again, this time onto a compass bearing of 325°. The reason for the change was another radar contact – this time a friendly one. At 10:20 hours the four warships of Commander Fisher's 36th Destroyer Division appeared off the port quarter, which meant that Burnett's Force 1 had now officially made contact with Convoy JW 55B and its escorts. However, at the same

Day 7: Sunday 26 December 1943

moment, the radar operators on the three British cruisers lost contact with the *Scharnhorst*.

The first skirmish of the Battle of North Cape was therefore something of a draw, or even a German tactical victory. Burnett had clearly been outmanoeuvred, but at least the *Scharnhorst* had been prevented from breaking through to the convoy. Critics have since argued that Bey should have fought his way past the three British cruisers. After all, he outgunned them, and his battlecruiser was significantly better armoured than Burnett's three cruisers. But this flew in the face of established German doctrine, which saw capital ships as being too valuable to be placed at risk, especially if such a risk was unnecessary. To the Kriegsmarine, battleships and battlecruisers were strategic rather than tactical assets – in the parlance of seapower, they were 'a force in being' that tied down enemy resources. The British had both the ships and the doctrine to place their battleships in harm's way – in fact, it was expected of them. Konter-Admiral Bey viewed things very differently. To avoid battle might involve losing political face in Germany but it preserved Germany's fleet.

Certainly, everyone on board the *Scharnhorst* had been taken by surprise that morning. Petty Officer Wilhelm Gödde, stationed on the port searchlight platform, told how the star shell was followed by enemy salvos – huge columns of water being thrown up on the port beam, a few hundred metres away from the ship. He recalled: 'They were caused by heavy shells. I couldn't see the ship that was firing at us – all I saw were the orange flashes every time a new salvo was fired.' Signaller Wilhelm Kruse was on the bridge at the time, and claimed that the officers identified just one enemy cruiser through darkness and driving snow. Gunner Günther Sträter added: 'Of the enemy, only the muzzle flashes could be seen, bearing 245°.'

The crew reacted quickly, the result of years of training together for just such an eventuality. One survivor claimed that turret 'Caesar' managed to return fire within a few minutes, while Kruse claimed that the surface radar was sending sighting reports to the bridge during these crucial few minutes. As soon as the enemy began firing, Kapitän-zur-See Hintze took all the correct steps to avoid being hit, and to distance his vessel from the enemy. But he was unable to avoid one of the British salvos. As Commander Welby-Everard suspected, the *Scharnhorst* was hit by the *Norfolk*'s third salvo.

The Battle of North Cape

One shell landed on the port side of the upper deck just behind the funnel, and just astern of a twin 5.9-inch gun mount. The 8-inch shell penetrated the upper deck and landed in a seamen's messdeck beneath it, next to a technical office. The shell didn't explode, but it started a fire, which was soon extinguished. A second shell hit the foremast, where Gunner Helmut Backhaus had a narrow escape:

> That shot was a lucky one. I was at my post on the upper platform and felt the draught when the shell whistled right over me. One man was killed, a lieutenant lost his foot, and several men were lightly wounded. When I struggled to my feet I saw what had happened.

The 8-inch shell had destroyed the forward Seetakt 'mattress' radar aerial and damaged the port high angle control system, used to direct anti-aircraft fire. The loss of the radar was a serious blow, as it severely limited the ability of the *Scharnhorst* to see through the darkness. True, the battlecruiser had a second aerial mounted further aft, but it had a limited sweep, and an effective range of less than 6 nautical miles.

By 09:45 hours it was clear that the enemy had ceased fire. Bey and Hintze could concentrate on working out what to do next. Bey sent a signal to Johannesson, requesting a position and update. He then gave the order to turn the battlecruiser round onto a north-easterly course, steering 045°. Ten minutes later, at 09:55 hours, the flotilla commander replied: 'Proceeding according to plan. Square AC4413. Course 230°. Speed 12 knots.' That was probably the moment that Bey realised his mistake – that his destroyer escorts had never been told to change course, either because the signal was never sent or he simply forgot to tell them. So far things had gone badly wrong for Bey: he had managed to become detached from his destroyers, he was ambushed by a powerful force of enemy cruisers, and he was now heading away from where he suspected the convoy might be. It was time for him to put things right.

First, Bey sent a signal to Peters in Narvik: 'Under fire from probable cruiser with radar.' When the signal was passed to General-admiral Schniewind in Kiel it would be his first proper confirmation that the *Scharnhorst* had begun her attack on the convoy, and that the

Day 7: Sunday 26 December 1943

suspected British covering force was actually in the same area. Hintze then made an announcement over the tannoy to his ship's company: 'Lull in action. We are trying once more to get at the convoy, the destroyers from the south, we in the *Scharnhorst* from the north.' If this was true, then it showed just how quickly Bey had reacted to the situation. However, Bey's cavalier disregard for his destroyer escort just 90 minutes earlier makes this suggestion of his following some greater plan a little suspicious. More likely Bey realised his mistake and was now trying to make the most of a bad situation.

His earlier reversal of course to the south, shortly before the start of the skirmish, may have been a belated attempt to regain contact with the destroyer escorts before continuing in search of the convoy. However, that plan had now changed, as Force 1 lay between the Battlegroup and its target. For his part, Johannesson must have realised something was amiss when he saw the glow to the north-east, but he stayed on course for another thirty minutes rather than using his initiative and turning towards the light, or even breaking radio silence and asking for instructions. As the minutes continued to tick by the destroyers remained on their old course.

Then, at 10:02, the *Scharnhorst* intercepted a radio message from Kapitänleutnant Lübsen in *U-277* to Peters in Narvik. Just over thirty minutes earlier he spotted the convoy, which was now heading east, to link up with Force 1. Because of the increased risk of collision in the mountainous seas, Rear Admiral Boucher had ordered his ships to display their navigation lights – a sensible precaution but also a risk. Lübsen spotted the lights to the north-east at 09:25 hours. After making sure he avoided the escorts he sent his message: Came suddenly upon the convoy ... Square AB6365, estimated course 90°.' Unknown to Bey, Lübsen had been navigating by dead reckoning for days, and his navigation was less than perfect. The position he gave was wrong – the real position was about 30 miles to the west-south-west. The navigation lights he saw were also not from the convoy, but from the escorts – Fisher's 36th Destroyer Division. They spotted the U-boat on the surface and opened fire, forcing *U-277* to submerge. As Fisher recalled:

I was some five miles astern (from the rest of his destroyers), putting down a shadowing U-boat when my division was again detached to join Bob Burnett's cruisers after their first brush with the *Scharnhorst*, and ran north with him at high speed in appalling weather, with the sea astern.

The result was that, while *U-277* was about 25 miles north-west of the *Scharnhorst*, Bey now placed the U-boat about 40 miles away to the north-east. The sighting convinced Bey that he could work his way around the British cruisers to attack the convoy from a different direction. At 10:27 hours he finally ordered Johannesson to turn his destroyers around and steer a course of 070° at a top speed of 25 knots. By that time the *Scharnhorst* was already steering 045°. While this meant that the two components of the German Battlegroup were now heading in the same general direction, it also meant that the *Scharnhorst* was still drawing further away from her escorts.

Kapitän-zur-See Hintze's announcement may have revealed the reasoning behind Bey's order to Johannesson. Before the U-boat report Bey was planning to work his way around Force 1, in order to fall on the convoy from the north-east. If he had thought the situation through he might have decided to ignore the U-boat report and rely instead on earlier, older estimates of Convoy JW 55B's position. Until Lübsen's signal he suspected the convoy lay 30 to 50 nautical miles away to the north-west, but he could not be sure. His destroyer sweep had revealed nothing, but the protective way that Burnett's cruisers had behaved should have suggested that his suspicions were correct. Burnett had obviously been screening something. By sending his destroyers so far to the south-west, Bey may have been covering his options. A sweep from there towards the north-west would have set Johannesson in the general direction of the convoy's real location. That might have explained why Bey prevaricated after Johannesson sent him his latest position. It would be half an hour before he gave the orders that turned the destroyers around. Konter-Admiral Bey should have trusted his instincts. That morning though, Bey wasn't the only admiral having second thoughts. At 10.35 hours Rear Admiral Burnett sent a signal to Admiral Fraser, reporting, 'Have lost touch with enemy who was steering north. Am closing convoy.' This was sent just over half an hour after his turn away from the *Scharnhorst* and fifteen minutes after the German battlecruiser disappeared from the radar screens of the British cruisers. This was the first Admiral

Day 7: Sunday 26 December 1943

Fraser knew that his prey had not only been sighted but engaged. It also meant that Konter-Admiral Bey had managed to evade his clutches. The decision to break contact had been a sound one but Fraser was unable to hide his disappointment. Within half an hour Burnett received a signal from Fraser, stating plainly that: 'Unless touch can be regained by some unit, there is no chance of my finding enemy.'

After the battle Burnett's decision to break contact was criticised in some quarters, but Fraser was well aware that his subordinate was simply doing what he had been ordered – placing the safety of the convoy in his charge above the more elusive prospects of bringing the *Scharnhorst* to battle. No lesser commander than Grossadmiral Dönitz supported the decision, writing: 'when *Scharnhorst* first turned away south and then turned north again, not to follow, but to close the convoy with his three cruisers in order to be able to protect it in the event of further attack by the *Scharnhorst*, was undoubtedly correct.' Burnett later gave his own reasoning: 'I was convinced he was trying to work round to the northward of the convoy, and in view of the limit on my speed imposed by the weather I decided to return to place myself between him and the convoy.' He added: 'I did not immediately alter course to port, as I wished to place Force 1 between the enemy and the convoy should he break away to the west and north, further to gain what advantage there was in the light.' He knew that the German battlecruiser was considerably faster and better placed than his own cruisers and simply made his decision based on common sense.

Fraser himself later supported his subordinate, stating that Burnett had reached the right decision in the circumstances, as did Captain Roskill, the Royal Navy's official historian of the battle, who declared that, after studying all the evidence, he thought it extremely unlikely the British cruisers could have continued to shadow the *Scharnhorst* by radar, given the battlecruiser's speed and the appalling weather conditions. He concluded that: 'criticism of Admiral Burnett's actions can therefore hardly be sustained.' If Burnett could be accused of anything, it was his uncharacteristic failure to deploy his ships correctly after the radar contact had first been established. But this was a minor tactical error – his operational and strategic decisions had been sound.

The Battle of North Cape

Moreover, Burnett would certainly make up for that tactical lapse when he next encountered the enemy.

In the meantime, Fraser's signal caused Burnett to doubt his own competency. He turned to his Flag Captain, Freddie Parham for support. Parham recalls being called to the *Belfast*'s chart room, where the Rear Admiral was coordinating the battle:

> When he'd taken his decision and settled down to keep with the convoy, he sent for me. He was down in the chart-house, one deck below the bridge. He himself worked entirely from the plot. I don't know that he ever came to the bridge at all. There was nothing to be seen from the bridge, it was pitch dark all the time. He left all that to me. He sent for me ... I went down, and he'd cleared the chart-house of everybody else. He said to me, 'Freddie, have I done the right thing?' I said to him, 'I'm absolutely certain you have.'
>
> Shortly after that we had a fairly snorting signal from the C-in-C which said, roughly speaking, 'if nobody keeps their eye on the *Scharnhorst*, how the hell do you think I'm going to bring her to action?' or words to that effect. It was a terrible thing. Poor old Bob, he was a terribly emotional chap, he was jolly nearly in tears about it. I was able to reassure him. And afterwards of course his judgement was proved utterly correct because the *Scharnhorst* turned up again to look for the convoy and ran straight into us. There is no question in my mind that Bob was right, absolutely right.

Afterwards, Parham added:

> In my humble opinion it was a brilliant decision. Our job essentially was to protect the convoy. Almost secondarily our job was to sink the *Scharnhorst* or anybody who came to interfere with the convoy. There is no doubt in my mind that if he had gone off and tried to find the *Scharnhorst* he would have lost her and he would not have protected the convoy.

As the time ticked by during that late morning, Burnett and his flag captain may have reached the right strategic decision, but they knew

Scharnhorst ever onward! The *Scharnhorst* in a heavy sea, painted by the German naval artist Bock, and presented to a former captain as a leaving present. Postcards of the painting were often given away as mementoes by the *Scharnhorst's* officers. (*Stratford Archive*)

The *Scharnhorst*, showing her disruptive paint scheme, which was designed to confound Allied visual rangefinders by giving the impression of her being a much shorter vessel. No amount of paint could hide her powerful armament or disguise her graceful lines. (*Stratford Archive*)

The foredeck of the *Scharnhorst*, with a covering of ice during operations in the Baltic Sea in the first winter of the war. Conditions beyond the Arctic Circle in late December were much worse. (*Stratford Archive*)

HMS *Duke of York* was one of a class of five battleships of the 'King George V' class, although her sister ship, HMS *Prince of Wales*, had been sunk in the Far East some two years earlier. During the battle she flew the flag of Admiral Fraser. (*Stratford Archive*)

The forward main turrets of HMS *Duke of York*. Her ten 14-inch guns were mounted in three turrets, two forward and one aft. The fire of these guns could be directed by either visual means or by radar. (*Stratford Archive*)

HMS *Duke of York* suffered only superficial damage during the battle. In this photograph a sailor is pictured examining shrapnel damage to the tripod structure of her lower foremast. (*Stratford Archive*)

The British destroyer HMS *Onslow* was typical of the escorts that protected the two Allied convoys, or which formed the striking force of the 36th Destroyer Division. In December 1943 the *Onslow* was commanded by Captain James McCoy, the commander of the escort force attached to Convoy JW 55B. (*Stratford Archive*)

The Enigma code machine was first invented in 1923, and the Germans regarded the messages it produced as being impossible to decipher. Unbeknown to the Kriegsmarine the British had successfully broken the Enigma codes, and during the campaign against the *Scharnhorst* the Admiralty were therefore able to provide Admiral Fraser with highly reliable and up-to-date intelligence reports. (*Stratford Archive*)

The depth-charging of a German U-boat during the Atlantic Campaign. During its progress through the Barents Sea, Convoy JW 55A was shadowed by German U-boats, and on two occasions the escorts located and tried to sink some of the enemy craft. (*Stratford Archive*)

The crew of a U-boat in Arctic waters, photographed beside their ice-covered 88mm deck gun. The limited battery power available to the Type VIIC U-boats meant that the boats had to spend most of their patrol time on the surface. (*Stratford Archive*)

A bridge watch on a U-boat during a patrol in rough seas. The men of Gruppe Eisenbart were primarily used as a reconnaissance force, but if the Allied convoy was located they were also expected to attack it. (*Stratford Archive*)

A signalman on the upper bridge of the *Scharnhorst*, signalling to the battlecruiser's sister ship, the *Gneisenau*, during a training cruise in the Baltic Sea soon after the start of the war. The sleek and graceful lines of the German battlecruisers made them some of the most attractive warships of the Second World War. (*Stratford Archive*)

German engine room artificers, pictured at their posts in the engine room of a German warship during action stations. Although the engine room staff of the *Scharnhorst* did their best, they were unable to prevent the battlecruiser from losing power during her final engagement, which in turn allowed Admiral Fraser's warships to catch up with her. (*Stratford Archive*)

Loading 11-inch shells on board the German battlecruiser. While the firepower of the *Scharnhorst* gave her a distinct edge over the cruisers of Force 1, she was outgunned by the *Duke of York*, and was therefore forced to rely on her speed and armour to escape. (*Stratford Archive*)

The *Scharnhorst*, pictured from the deck of her sister ship, the *Gneisenau*, during the 'Channel Dash' of February 1942. Her success during this operation earned her the reputation of being a lucky ship. In this photograph she is preceded by the *Prinz Eugen*. (*Stratford Archive*)

The *Tirpitz*, anchored in the Altenfjord, surrounded by attendant vessels and anti-submarine defences. In the weeks preceding the *Scharnhorst*'s last sortie, the German battleship was undergoing repairs and was therefore not available for offensive operations. (*Stratford Archive*)

After Fraser's ships reached Murmansk the survivors of the *Scharnhorst* were transferred to the *Duke of York*, for transport to Britain. Fraser ignored Soviet requests that they be handed over to the Soviet Navy for interrogation. (*Stratford Archive*)

Generaladmiral Otto Schniewind was the Fleet Commander of the Kriegsmarine, and was therefore Konter-Admiral Bey's direct superior. His reluctance to advise Grossadmiral Dönitz to call off Operation Ostfront meant that Bey and his men were forced to embark on an operation for which they were ill-prepared. (*Stratford Archive*)

Survivors of the *Scharnhorst* were transported to Scapa Flow, where they began their journey into prisoner-of-war camps. These men were eventually sent to camps in Canada and the United States. (*Stratford Archive*)

The German yacht *Grille* ('Cricket'), which was used as a floating headquarters, berthed in Narvik. It was from her that Kapitän-zur-See Peters maintained a link between Bey's Battlegroup, the U-boats of Gruppe Eisenbart, and German Naval Headquarters in Kiel. (*Stratford Archive*)

A convoy gathered in Loch Ewe, viewed from a merchantman anchored near its western shore. The mountains of Wester Ross can be seen in the background, beyond the eastern shore of the sea loch. (*Stratford Archive*)

German 'Narvik' class destroyer Z-33, photographed at anchor in the Langefjord before she sailed in company with the *Scharnhorst* in December 1943. During the operation she was commanded by Kapitän-zur-See Erich Holtorf. (*Stratford Archive*)

The quarterdeck of the *Scharnhorst*, viewed during a brief foray into Arctic waters from beneath 'Dora' turret. During the final battle this after turret remained in operation until it ran out of ammunition. (*Stratford Archive*)

The *Scharnhorst* in heavy seas, photographed during her foray into the Atlantic Ocean in company with the *Gneisenau*. Her radars were located on top of her forward and after gunnery direction towers. (*Stratford Archive*)

Rear Admiral Robert Burnett, photographed in his cabin on board HMS *Belfast*. It was his cruisers that made first contact with the *Scharnhorst*, and after protecting the convoy they shadowed her until the enemy battlecruiser could be brought to battle by Admiral Fraser. (*Stratford Archive*)

Admiral Bruce Fraser was a highly intelligent commander and a specialist in naval gunnery, who planned the interception of the *Scharnhorst* and engineered her destruction. (*Stratford Archive*)

Commander Ralph Fisher, the commander of the 36th Destroyer Division, who flew his pennant in HMS *Musketeer*. It was his destroyers that finally finished off the German battlecruiser. (*Stratford Archive*)

Konter-Admiral Erich Bey was a small-ship commander, and he never appeared comfortable commanding the capital ships of the Northern Battlegroup. He was also ordered to sortie against the Arctic convoys with little chance to prepare for the operation. (*Stratford Archive*)

Kapitän-zur-See Fritz Hintze was a highly experienced and well respected naval officer, and during Operation Ostfront he handled his ship with commendable skill. (*Stratford Archive*)

Grossadmiral Karl Dönitz and his staff. Operation Ostfront came about because he promised Hitler that the Kriegsmarine would do what it could to help the war effort on the Eastern front. (*Stratford Archive*)

The *Tirpitz, Admiral Scheer* and *Admiral Hipper* on exercise in Norwegian waters. The Northern Battlegroup remained a latent force to be reckoned with, but by late 1943 its power had been greatly eroded by damage and redeployment. (*Stratford Archive*)

HMS *Belfast*, the flagship of Rear Admiral Burnett. She is the only ship from the battle that is still afloat, and she now functions as a floating museum, moored in the River Thames beside London Bridge. (*Stratford Archive*)

Captain Addis's HMS *Sheffield* took part in the first two skirmishes between Force 1 and the *Scharnhorst*, but mechanical problems prevented her from participating in the final stage of the battle. (*Stratford Archive*)

HMS *Jamaica* regarded herself as the *Duke of York*'s 'shadow', and during the final battle she followed in the wake of the battleship, adding the firepower of her twelve 6-inch guns to the weight of British fire. (*Stratford Archive*)

The heavy cruiser HMS *Norfolk* was the most powerful warship in Rear Admiral Burnett's Force 1, although she was still hopelessly outgunned by the *Scharnhorst*. (*Stratford Archive*)

Two small 'Flower' class corvettes formed part of the escort of Convoy JW 55B, while three more helped protect the homebound Convoy RA 55A. These tiny, storm-tossed warships played a vital part in protecting their charges from enemy U-boats. (*Stratford Archive*)

'Tribal' class destroyers such as HMS *Ashanti* were powerful, fast, and well-armed. Unfortunately, they were used to protect the two convoys, rather than forming part of the force that brought the *Scharnhorst* to bay. *Ashanti* formed part of the escort force attached to Convoy RA 55A. (*Stratford Archive*)

HMS *Duke of York*, photographed during her triumphant return to Scapa Flow on New Year's Day, 1944. She and the other returning warships that took part in the battle were cheered by the rest of the fleet. (*Stratford Archive*)

A German sailor, calling out to be rescued from the sea. This young U-boat crewman was fortunate – his vessel didn't sink in the Barents Sea in December, at night, and in the middle of a gale. (*Stratford Archive*)

Admiral Fraser and his captains, photographed on the deck of HMS *Duke of York* in Scapa Flow in early 1944. From right to left: Capt. Russell (*Duke of York*), Cdr. Lee-Barber (*Opportune*), Cdr. Fisher (*Musketeer*), Lt. Cdr. Storheill (*Stord*), Cdr. Meyrick (*Savage*), Admiral Fraser, Capt. Hughes-Hallett (*Jamaica*), Lt. Cdr. Walmsley (*Saumarez*), Lt. Cdr. Clouston (*Scorpion*) and Lt. Shaw (*Matchless*). (*Stratford Archive*)

Day 7: Sunday 26 December 1943

Fraser had a point: until contact was regained with the *Scharnhorst* then the whole course of the battle hung in the balance. That morning the minutes must have passed with agonising slowness for the two British admirals. Burnett elaborated on his reasoning in his official report to Fraser after the battle:

> Considering my chief object to be the safe and timely arrival of the convoy and being convinced I should shortly make contact again, it would not have been correct tactics to have left the merchant ships during daylight to search for the enemy, nor to have split my force by detaching one or more ships to search, in view of the enemy's high speed and the weather conditions which limited a cruiser to 24 knots. Feeling confident that the enemy would return to the attack from the north or north-east, and keeping in mind the object of the operation, I decided to carry out a broad zigzag about 10 miles ahead of the convoy. *Musketeer*, *Matchless*, *Opportune* and *Virago* were disposed ahead as screen.

He had made his dispositions, and Burnett knew there was now little he could do but to wait for the *Scharnhorst* to reappear.

Meanwhile, Admiral Fraser had other problems apart from maintaining contact with the *Scharnhorst*. At the same moment as Force 1 lost contact with the *Scharnhorst*, the Germans finally managed to spot Force 2. Shortly after 9:00 hours, a flight of three BV-138 flying boats took off from Bardufoss airfield, near Tromsø, and then headed north. These were strange-looking aircraft, powered by three engines, and with a twin tail. However, they had a range of almost 2,500 miles, they could often fly in bad weather, and above all they were equipped with Fug-200 Hohentweil radars, which gave them a surface search range of approximately 20 nautical miles. Officially the Luftwaffe called these flying boats 'Sea Dragons'. The six-men crews of these lumbering aircraft preferred the name 'Flying Clogs'.

The three aircraft spread into a line when they reached Point Lucie, which marked the entrance into the Altenfjord. Twenty minutes later, at 10:10 hours, Lieutenant Helmut Marx, commanding the most westerly of the three flying boats picked up a contact on radar. He waited a couple of minutes while his navigator checked the position, and then sent a radio message back to Bardufoss: 'Several vessels located', followed by the grid square. He and his companions continued to shadow the ships for another ninety minutes, sending regular reports throughout the morning. During these reports he identified one of the contacts as being 'large' – a sure sign of a battleship or aircraft carrier. On board the *Duke of York* Admiral Fraser knew that Force 2 had been spotted but there was little he could do. British radar operators tracked the aircraft until 12:30 hours, during which time they maintained position about 8 miles to the south of the British force, off its starboard quarter. During this time the battleship picked up radio signals from one of the aircraft, which confirmed that the ships had been sighted.

One of the great mysteries of the battle is why this crucial sighting report wasn't transmitted immediately to Admiral Bey on board the *Scharnhorst*. In fact, the intelligence staff at Bardufoss must have questioned the accuracy of Lieutenant Marx's report, as it took more than an hour for the information to be confirmed, then passed to General Roth, the senior Luftwaffe commander in northern Norway. It was after 13:40 hours that Roth's staff passed the information to Kapitän-zur-See Peters in Narvik. During those crucial three and a half hours Force 2 continued to steer a course to the west (080°) at a speed of 25 knots. If Bey had known of the sighting report immediately, then he would have been able to extricate himself from the trap. Instead, the Luftwaffe did nothing and Lieutenant Marx's efforts were wasted.

Although Peters had no sighting report to pass on that morning, he did receive disquieting reports of more enemy radio traffic from the vicinity of the Barents Sea. German radio direction-finding equipment had first detected a transmission at 09:40 hours that morning – a report from Burnett reporting his contact with the *Scharnhorst*. Peters presumed it was sent to his headquarters in Scapa Flow, but it could also have been destined for another naval force. Then a few minutes later another signal was intercepted. It had just been sent from naval transmitter codenamed 'DGO' to another naval force. This was actually a signal from Admiral Fraser to Captain McCoy in HMS *Onslow*, ordering him to detach four destroyers to join Force 1. At German Naval Headquarters in Kiel these intercept reports were logged, then passed to Peters in Narvik. For some reason the same

Day 7: Sunday 26 December 1943

reports were never forwarded to Admiral Bey. Shortly after 11:00 hours Admiral Schniewind conceded that:

> The reporting from one British unit to another could have been addressed to the convoy from a cruiser, but may equally have been a direction of the supposed heavy cover force towards the target.

However, he was unwilling to recall the *Scharnhorst* without clearer information. So far there was nothing that confirmed the presence of anything other than Burnett's cruisers and the convoy in the Barents Sea. However, to Kapitän-zur-See Peters in Narvik, the report of these transmissions was an ominous sign, suggesting a second covering force somewhere out there in the darkness.

The signal that caused the alarm was sent by Admiral Fraser to Captain McCoy as a direct consequence of Burnett's encounter with the *Scharnhorst*. At 09:30 hours the admiral had already ordered the convoy to steer to the north – away from the possible location of the German Battlegroup – an order sent minutes after Force 1 opened fire on the enemy. With Convoy JW 55B now heading out of harm's way, Fraser decided to use McCoy's Fighting Destroyer Escort to reinforce Burnett's cruisers. After all, in a battle where visibility was reduced to a few miles, these destroyers could easily work their way within range of the enemy ship before launching a crippling spread of torpedoes. At 09:37 hours the order was given to detach four destroyers. McCoy selected his most obvious candidates, the four vessels of Commander Fisher's 36th Division.

Actually, McCoy had anticipated the order as soon as he saw the star shell. He had already radioed Burnett's flagship, asking if the admiral wanted destroyer reinforcements. Fraser's orders simply confirmed matters. Fisher had already moved into position between the convoy and the *Scharnhorst*, driving off one enemy U-boat – Kapitänleutnant Lübsen's *U-277*. Fisher described the problems facing his four destroyers as they steamed off at high speed through the mountainous seas. The destroyers were almost unmanageable and

[in] danger of broaching. In fact, Johnny Lee-Barber, a much more experienced destroyer captain than I, signalled that it was

impossible to go on at that speed. However, we did without serious mishap.

Force 1 had already picked up the extreme eastern end of Fisher's destroyer screen on radar around 09:10 hours. This was the contact that caused Burnett and his staff a few anxious moments until they worked out that the contacts were heading north, and were therefore part of the convoy. It took Fisher's destroyers the best part of thirty minutes to work their way eastward towards Force 1, but the two groups of ships finally sighted each other at 10:20 hours. That was also the moment when the *Scharnhorst* finally disappeared off the British radar screens. Burnett expected the German battlecruiser to reappear any minute and he was clearly on edge. It was exactly the wrong moment for Commander Fisher to ask his superior for instructions. The destroyer commander recalled the incident later:

> I had never been in company with Bob Burnett before and was at this time wondering what was to be the form about destroyers attacking, so I made the signal . . . carefully worded so that there was no need for him to reply in the event that we met the enemy before he could do so.

The signal read: 'Intend to await your order before leading destroyers to attack.' Given the circumstances it is hardly surprising that Burnett and his staff misinterpreted this confusing signal. Had Fisher spotted the *Scharnhorst*? Was he about to attack something? By the time the signal reached Burnett it had been shortened by the chief yeoman and now read: 'Am awaiting your order to attack.' Even Captain Parham of the *Belfast* admitted that:

> I was very puzzled. I could just see *Musketeer*'s Division, and only just – beyond them – the convoy. I reported the signal down the voice-pipe to my admiral, adding that I could not understand it: I could see no sign of *Scharnhorst* and, if she were there, surely *Musketeer* would not wait for an order to attack.

Burnett ordered Parham to respond with the signal 'Attack what?' Within seconds the disarming reply came back from HMS *Musketeer*: 'Anything that turns up!'

Day 7: Sunday 26 December 1943

Once this problem had been sorted out the newly-reinforced Force 1 continued on a course of 325°, and at 10:50 hours radar operators on board *Norfolk* picked up contacts to the north-north-west, bearing 324°, at a range of 14 nautical miles. It was the convoy. At this point it was steering 045° at a speed of 8 knots, and so Burnett's cruisers raced forward to take station ahead. Burnett ordered Fisher's destroyers to form a screen a mile ahead of the cruisers. This time, if the *Scharnhorst* made another appearance, it would have to fight its way through Burnett to reach the convoy. An hour earlier Fraser had ordered the convoy to steer north, in an attempt to put as much distance as it could between it and the *Scharnhorst*. Then, at 10:30, Fraser ordered the convoy to revert to its original course of 045°. Any course change involving the wayward merchant ships of Convoy JW 55B was a difficult process, and changes had to be made in small increments to avoid complete confusion. Consequently, the convoy had barely settled onto its new course when Force 1 appeared.

Confusion seemed to be in the air that morning. At 11:30 hours one of McCoy's destroyers – HMS *Onslaught* – reported a radar contact on a bearing of 150°. For a few minutes McCoy thought it might be the *Scharnhorst*, until the contact sent the signal: '*Onslaught* from CS10: *Onslaught*'s unknown radio contact is me.' The 'CS10' stood for Burnett himself, the commander of the 10th Cruiser Squadron. Minutes later radar operators on board *Norfolk* thought they detected something to the north-east, but the contact proved to be another false alarm.

Both Fraser and Burnett now had to face the reality that the *Scharnhorst* could be anywhere. The German battlecruiser had last been seen heading off towards the north-east, but with her superior speed she could easily work her way around the convoy and attack from the north, or even the north-west. Worse still was the possibility she wouldn't attack the convoy at all – that the whole operation had been a gigantic bluff. She could just as easily have slipped past both Force 1 and the convoy, and at that moment might be steaming west at full speed, having slipped through the British net. If so, nothing lay between her and the Atlantic, where she could play havoc with the Atlantic convoys. Force 2 was heading in the wrong direction to intercept, and anyway, the *Duke of York* and the *Jamaica* lacked the fuel to give chase deep into the Atlantic without pausing to refuel.

The Battle of North Cape

As the clock ticked towards noon, the two British admirals could do nothing but wait.

However, to guard against an attack from the north, Fraser ordered Boucher and McCoy to use their discretion to keep Convoy JW 55B from danger. Consequently, at 11:55 hours, Boucher gave the order that would gradually swing the convoy round onto a new course of 125° – a south-easterly heading. Force 1 continued to operate to the north-east of the convoy but altered course in order to maintain its relative position. After all, it was the blocking force, designed to cover the most likely avenue of German attack. It was hoped that this would be enough to keep the convoy safe, at least until the *Scharnhorst* was sighted. The truth was, while the British expected the *Scharnhorst* to appear from the north-east, nobody really knew where she was, or from which direction Konter-Admiral Bey planned to strike.

The Afternoon Watch (12:00–15:59 hours)

Noon should have brought a respite, a time when the crews of both sides changed watches and ate a meal at their action stations. Of course, what hot food was available was produced in raging seas, and had to be transported to the men wherever they were – in gun turrets, engine rooms and on the open deck. On board the *Duke of York* one sailor described his lunch that day as: 'the most god-awful action messing dinner – a fatty stew – virtually uneatable.' Lieutenant Leach in 'A' turret described the same meal as 'lumps of soggy pork swilling in fannies full of greasy sludge.' The lucky ones, like Lieutenant Ramsden, on board the *Jamaica*, were handed sandwiches. Nobody on board the *Scharnhorst* recalled what was served up, but the crew had remained at action stations all morning and would have eaten anything, however badly cooked it might have been.

But conditions would have been uncomfortable. Around 11:40 hours the *Scharnhorst* turned from her northerly course onto a new heading of 225° (south-west). That meant she was now sailing directly into the gale, making conditions extremely unpleasant for her crew. Konter-Admiral Bey was now making a second attack run on the convoy, heading directly toward its estimated position. His signal to Kapitän-zur-See Johannesson, just before noon, showed what he planned to do. By ordering the destroyers to 'Operate towards Square AB6365'

Day 7: Sunday 26 December 1943

he planned to attack the convoy from two sides – the destroyers from the south and the *Scharnhorst* from the north-east.

On board the *Scharnhorst*, a little before noon, Kapitän-zur-See Hintze announced:

> From the Captain to all stations: Situation report. As expected, this morning we encountered the convoy's covering force – three 'Town' class cruisers. We have changed course, and are attempting to attack the convoy from the opposite side – from the north. We have shaken off the cruisers.

The only problem was that Convoy JW 55B was some distance to the north of where Bey expected it to be. However, to the east-south-east of the convoy was Force 1, placed to cover what Rear Admiral Burnett suspected to be the most likely avenue of approach for the German battlecruiser. When the battle resumed, Force 1 was therefore ideally placed to prevent the *Scharnhorst* from attacking the convoy.

With the benefit of hindsight, Grossadmiral Dönitz saw this as the moment when the operation began to unravel – 'tactical coordination between *Scharnhorst* and the 4th Destroyer Flotilla had therefore ceased to exist'. This wasn't strictly true. By this stage Bey and Johannesson were in radio contact with each other and were trying to coordinate their actions. However, Dönitz had a convenient scapegoat in Konter-Admiral Bey, and he seemed in no mood to excuse the Battlegroup commander. As he saw it, Force 1 was no match for the *Scharnhorst*, which was: 'far superior to them in armour, sea-keeping qualities and, above all, in firepower.' Dönitz argued that Bey should have engaged Force 1 more aggressively during the first encounter 'When contact had been established in the morning, the ensuing gun battle should have been fought out to its conclusion.' Once the British cruisers had been sunk, disabled or severely damaged, then the convoy would have no defences save a few destroyers. Consequently, the convoy would have fallen into Bey's hands 'like ripe fruit'. But this was merely speculation. Bey was obeying current German naval doctrine when he broke contact, and by returning to the fray he was demonstrating that he had more than enough aggressive spirit to achieve the naval victory Dönitz so desperately needed.

The Battle of North Cape

At 12:04 hours, this period of uncertainty and frustration came to an end. That was when the operators of the Type 273Q radar on board HMS *Belfast* picked up a new 'jig' type to the east-north-east, at a range of 26,000 yards. There was little doubt what this mystery contact would be. *Belfast* immediately made the signal: 'Jig 075 – 13' – shorthand for an unknown radar contact on a bearing of 075° and at a range of 13 nautical miles. At the time the three cruisers of Force 1 were in line astern, with *Belfast* in the lead, followed by *Sheffield*, then the *Norfolk*. The four destroyers of the 36th Destroyer Division were also formed into line astern, two miles ahead of the cruisers, off the *Belfast*'s starboard bow. *Musketeer* was in the lead, followed by *Matchless*, *Opportune* and *Virago*. The whole of Force 1 was steering a course of 045° at a speed of 18 knots. At the moment the *Scharnhorst* was detected the convoy lay some 9 miles to the west-north-west of Force 1, and at that moment was labouring round onto a new heading of 125°, at a speed of 7 knots.

When news of the contact was passed to Admiral Fraser in the *Duke of York*, his relief must have been evident. The Fleet Signals Officer Lieutenant Commander Courage recalled that:

> It was an electrifying moment. I was on the admiral's bridge by myself, and heads popped out from the plot. Turn 'em round again! Anyhow, we were all so pleased that we were about to get back into contact again.

The comment about turning Force 2 around stemmed from a brief reversal of course, ordered by Fraser just minutes before the radar contact was reported. The admiral had been concerned about the lack of any sighting of the German Battlegroup, and thought it prudent to move a little to the west, just in case the *Scharnhorst* was attempting to break out into the North Atlantic. The report ended the uncertainty and Force 2 was immediately ordered back onto its old course of 090°. Fraser was determined to place his battleship between the *Scharnhorst* and the safety of the Altenfjord. The admiral also realised that the odds had just tipped heavily in his favour. As he wrote in his diary: 'I knew now that there was every chance of catching the enemy.'

Seven minutes after the first radar sighting the *Sheffield* picked up the same radar contact, on a bearing of 075° and a range of 13 nautical miles. Three minutes later, at 12:14 hours, the *Norfolk* picked up the 'jig', which meant that the targeting information was now being fed to the guns of all three British cruisers. After tracking the contact for three minutes the *Sheffield* reported the 'jig' was now bearing 078°, at a range of 21,000 yards (10½ nautical miles), and three minutes after that, at 13:16 hours, the contact lay on a bearing of 094° at a range of 17,000 yards (8½ nautical miles). This told Burnett two things. First, the *Scharnhorst* was on an almost reciprocal course but was pulling away slightly to the right, which meant the enemy was steering a course of less than 255° (the reciprocal of the first radar bearing), so the two forces were virtually on collision course. The two forces were also approaching each other at a combined speed of about 40 knots. This meant that within fifteen minutes of first making radar contact *Belfast* would be around 15,000 yards away from the target. Normally there was little chance that her 6-inch Mk XXII guns could penetrate the armour of the German battlecruiser. However, when the range reduced to less than 12,000 yards the probability of causing a penetrating hit increased significantly. This time everything was working in favour of the British. To improve the angle of his guns Burnett ordered his cruisers to change course, first onto a heading of 090° at 12:16 hours, and then 100° three minutes later. This time there would be no chance that the line of fire would be blocked by other ships in the same force.

Rear Admiral Burnett gave the order to open fire at 12:21 hours, when the range had dropped to just 11,000 yards. Just as had happened earlier that morning, a star shell was fired to illuminate the target, followed by a full salvo of 6-inch shells. The star shell lit up the target and at a range of just 5½ miles the *Scharnhorst* was clearly visible from the bridge of the *Belfast*. As Captain Parham recalled: 'She looked extremely large, and extremely formidable.' *Sheffield* made the signal, 'Enemy in sight!', which was immediately passed to Force 1. Once again the Germans seem to have been taken completely by surprise – they had no idea the British cruisers were stalking them in the darkness. Burnett's gamble had paid off. His cruisers now lay between the *Scharnhorst* and the convoy, the enemy was taken unawares and was well within range of his cruisers' guns.

On the *Scharnhorst*, Seaman Sträter recalled that Kapitän-zur-See Hintze had only just exhorted the lookouts to keep a good watch when

The Battle of North Cape

the star shell burst overhead: 'Shortly afterwards the shadowy outlines of the British ships came into view.' By that time the battlecruiser was under fire from all three British cruisers and the leading two destroyers. Burnett ordered Commander Fisher's destroyers to attack with torpedoes, but for some reason the signal was never passed to the bridge of HMS *Musketeer*, and the opportunity slipped away. As Fisher later put it:

> I was anxiously awaiting the signal that would release me to split into two sub-divisions and attack with torpedoes from both her bows, but it never reached me. It came to light that the signal 'NS' (code for 'Destroyers attack with torpedoes') had in fact been received, but was never passed to the bridge by my harassed and tired signal staff who had otherwise done splendidly during the past two days.

In fairness, the angle was all wrong for a torpedo attack, and even Fisher later admitted that the battlecruiser 'did not present a useful torpedo target'. Lacking any other orders, Fisher ordered the *Musketeer* to open fire on the *Scharnhorst* at 12:22 with her forward 4.7-inch guns – a rather futile gesture given the armoured protection of the target. The range was now 7,000 yards and the *Scharnhorst* was steering straight towards them.

Behind the flotilla leader the *Matchless* joined in the firing. In the next fourteen minutes *Musketeer* alone fired fifty-two shells at the battlecruiser, some of which were fired at a range of 4,000 yards. Petty Officer Gödde, who was a lookout on board the battlecruiser, claims that none of the British shots actually hit the battlecruiser but several came close. This seems unlikely – another *Scharnhorst* survivor recalled that the ship was hit a little forward of 'Caesar' turret, and that the British fire was 'unpleasantly accurate', with shell fragments spraying the open decks.

The difference in these accounts may well be because Gödde was referring to hits that actually penetrated the armour of the ship, rather than exploding against her armoured hull and exposed superstructure. The gunners of HMS *Norfolk* claimed at least one hit at 12:24 hours, after three minutes of firing, and the flash from the hit was spotted by observers on board the *Belfast*. Similarly, the *Sheffield* also claimed at

Day 7: Sunday 26 December 1943

least one hit at 12:25 hours, the flash of which was spotted by her own observers. However, this fire seemed to inflict little or no damage on the enemy, whose own guns were able to bear on the British ships and open fire within a minute of the action starting. As one *Scharnhorst* survivor put it, as soon as they could be brought to bear, 'Turrets Anton and Bruno fired to starboard. After a change of course Caesar turret followed suit.' When the star shell burst over the ship Hintze ordered an immediate change of course to starboard, to throw off enemy gunnery. At this point she was heading on a course of roughly 270° or due west. Then, four minutes into the battle, at 12:25 hours, Hintze ordered the battlecruiser to turn hard to port, until she settled onto a new course of 135° (south-west). She was still making about 20 knots.

Nine miles away to the west the exchange of fire was witnessed by the men of Convoy JW 55B and her escorts. They saw the star shell bursting, on a bearing of 083°, followed by the flashes of gunfire. At that point the convoy escorts had only just finished shepherding their charges onto a new course of 125°, which meant that the fighting was now taking place off the port beam of the convoy. Captain McCoy reacted by ordering his escort destroyers to form up on the port side of the convoy, in two separate divisions. That way McCoy could throw his destroyers against the *Scharnhorst* if the German battlecruiser managed to force her way past Rear Admiral Burnett's warships. That might buy enough time for the convoy to escape into the darkness. However, their orders were to protect the convoy, not to steam off towards the gunfire. On board HMS *Onslaught* Commander 'Joe' Selby was a close friend of Rear Admiral Burnett, and Sub Lieutenant Carey remembered how he listened intently to the radio transmissions from Force 1:

> He followed the battle with personal sympathy as well as professional interest through a loud-speaker tuned in to the R/T signals from the cruisers which came in loud, clear, and in plain language now that radio silence was broken.

There was little Selby and his crew could do but listen to the sound of battle and wish they could intervene.

The Battle of North Cape

Beneath the *Belfast*'s 'A' turret, a gunner recalled the initial exchange of fire: 'The "Stand By" is given again. Then there is the most awful crash as our guns go off. I start taking shells from the trays and putting them on the shell ring round the three shell hoists. I repeat this operation every time the guns go off. Conversation starts again. "This is the first time this ship has fired her guns in anger." – "I wish they would tell us what we are firing at; anyway I hope it is nothing larger than a Destroyer." – "It's a pretty feeble enemy – it's not even firing back!" From the gun house comes a message, "Well done, A and B turrets; now give X and Y a chance." So we are one up on the Marines.' The firing lasts about twenty minutes.

At 12:25 hours, when the *Scharnhorst* made her dramatic alteration of course to port, the two sides were little more than 4,000 yards apart – just 2 nautical miles. This was point-blank range, even for the destroyers and light cruisers. The *Scharnhorst* was also hitting back. She straddled *Sheffield* with her first salvo, landing between the light cruiser and the *Norfolk*, and sweeping the starboard side of the *Sheffield* with scraps of shrapnel the size of a football. Lieutenant Walker, the *Sheffield*'s paymaster, was at his action station as fire direction officer of the 20mm pom-pom guns, mounted above the seaplane hangar. One piece of shrapnel, which Walker described as 'about the size of a man's head', penetrated the starboard side of the ship, just below and astern of the bridge, severing a steam pipe and several electrical cables. Fortunately, the steam heating pipe had been shut off when the cruiser went to action stations, and nobody was injured when it burst. Another large piece of shrapnel entered the starboard side of the hangar immediately below Walker. As a result of these glancing blows the upper deck of the *Sheffield* was covered in clouds of black, acrid smoke and fumes.

The *Scharnhorst* then concentrated her fire on the *Norfolk*, the most powerful of her main adversaries. The *Norfolk* was also using guns without flashless cordite, which meant that whenever her own 8-inch guns fired, the observers on board the *Scharnhorst* found their target fully illuminated. At 12:27 hours – four minutes after the *Scharnhorst* first returned fire – an 11-inch shell hit the *Norfolk*'s 'X' turret, penetrating its barbette mounting, damaging its traversing mechanism, and putting the turret out of action. On board the *Sheffield* Lieutenant Walker saw a 'sickening red column of fire', which hung over the stern

Day 7: Sunday 26 December 1943

of the *Norfolk* for about ten seconds before dying away. It was a clear indication that the cruiser had been badly hit. It could have been much worse, but quick thinking by the *Norfolk*'s crew meant that the magazine serving 'X' turret was flooded as a precaution against the spread of fire down from the turret itself. A minute later the *Norfolk* was hit again, and this time the 11-inch shot penetrated her weakly armoured deck amidships, exploding outside the cruiser's secondary damage control centre. This time the shell failed to hit the vitals of the ship, although it caused casualties. Warrant Mechanician Parini was killed outright, along with another petty officer and five other engine-room crew. Two more men later died of their wounds and three more were seriously injured.

Stoker Moth was one of the damage control party whose action station was just beside the centre of the explosion:

> Crash came the shell, about midships, starboard side, exploding in a compartment adjacent to my own. In the next two or three minutes there was inevitable confusion. Lights went out, and one of my mess-mates standing with his back to the communicating door was thrown across the deck by the blast from the explosion. The door was then opened. All was dark. Clouds of steam and smoke came issuing from within, along with cries for help, while a mixture of water and oil was rising slowly in the compartment below. I at once informed damage control headquarters: 'Shell inboard starboard side, exploding in the office flat.' The engine room forward repair parties, along with shipwrights and torpedo-men and damage control parties, were soon on the job, while the medical parties worked feverishly with our illfated casualties. Part of the shell exploded down the starboard engine-room hatch, causing a further two casualties.

At the same time, the *Norfolk*'s main type 273Q radar was put out of action, possibly by a smaller calibre German shell. In all, seven of her crew were killed during this exchange of fire and five more were seriously wounded.

Given that the *Norfolk* had been subjected to the point-blank fire of nine 11-inch guns, she escaped with remarkably little damage. She had been outclassed and outfought, but she survived the experience.

The Battle of North Cape

However, by that stage the real concern on board was for her engines. The shell that hit amidships had exploded directly above the engine room, and the engine spaces were filled with smoke and fumes. For several minutes there was a real worry that the engines themselves were damaged, and that a fire had started that would soon spread through the machinery spaces.

For some reason the secondary damage control centre passed on a message to Captain Bain on the bridge that the fires had been started above the engine room, and that they were now out of control. The ship was in danger unless speed was reduced. But the rumour was soon exposed, and as Captain Bain put it:

> The men in the engine room continued to give *Norfolk* more knots than she had ever had before and, instead of dropping back, we were there in the final phase of the action.

There could have been little better testimony to the crew of the *Norfolk* than their desire to stay in the fight until the end. Lieutenant Commander Reed, an engineer officer, recalled that the engine room crew simply put on their gas masks and continued to work as though nothing had happened. He recalled one nineteen-year-old rating, whose job was to record changes in boiler pressure: 'He just leaned on the rail in front of the indicator dials and recorded every movement for hours as if nothing had happened or was happening.'

An even more emotive testimony came from Chief Artificer Davies:

> We knew what we were up against, and set our minds on the engines so that we became quite unconscious of the passing of time. When the *Scharnhorst*'s shell tore in through the side of the ship and ripped up the deck just above us as if it were cardboard, we felt a terrific blast across the engine room. There was a thick pall of smoke from one corner of the engine room and a strong smell of burning; but we had 80,000 horse power to control and we had not much time to think of other things. Our ears were keyed for any strange noise in the engines, which might give us a first indication of trouble. Most of the men in the engine room were 'hostilities only' ratings. As an old R.N. man I can tell you they were something to be proud of. Not one faltered, and I

Day 7: Sunday 26 December 1943

suppose we were all, at the back of our minds, expecting something to happen any minute.

Chief Artificer Cansfield, in the after boiler room recalled that:

We had been closed up and in action for some time, and I was going to the forward boiler room when I saw a vivid green flame shoot across the ship, and the next minute one of the flats above the engine room was burning fiercely. I knew that the fire-fighting parties would deal with that, and went down to my action station again. The 'buzz' went round that we had been hit by another 11-inch shell, but I did not really know anything about that until it was all over and the *Scharnhorst* had been sunk.

Petty Officer Gödde provides us with a view of the action from the German perspective:

Shortly after 12:20 hours I and several other lookouts sighted three shadows ahead and reported accordingly. The alarm had already been sounded as the result of a previous radar contact. However, before our guns could open fire the first star shells were bursting over the *Scharnhorst*. The enemy's shells were falling pretty close to the ship. The first salvoes from our own main guns straddled the target. I myself observed that after three or four salvoes a large fire broke out close to the after funnel of one of the cruisers, while another cruiser was burning fiercely fore and aft and was enveloped in thick smoke.

After further salvoes I saw that the third cruiser had been hit in the bows. For a brief moment a huge pillar of flame shot up, and then died away. From the thick smoke surrounding her I presumed the ship was on fire. The enemy's fire then began to become more irregular. While we altered course the enemy cruisers turned away and disappeared in the rain and snow squalls. During this action the enemy had remained visible both ahead of us and on both sides. Both of our 'Anton' and 'Bruno' turrets had been firing, as had the two forward 15cm guns. I did not hear of any hits on the *Scharnhorst* being reported, either by telephone or by other means. The enemy had been scarcely visible during the first action, but this time, with the twilight of mid-day, their silhouettes were clearly distinguishable. Besides, our range was also much shorter than it had been in the morning.

The battle itself lasted just twenty minutes. After making her turn to the south-west the *Scharnhorst* increased speed to 28 knots, and although Force 1 tried its best to follow, it soon became clear that the German battlecruiser was getting away again. At 12:31 hours she had increased the range between herself and the *Belfast* to 12,400 yards; and ten minutes later, at 12:41 hours, the gap had increased to 13,000 yards (6½ nautical miles), on a bearing of 138°.

Commander Fisher's destroyers tried their best to keep up. At 12:31 hours they increased speed to 26 knots – the best they could manage in the conditions – and the cruisers themselves increased speed to 24 knots. But it was clearly a losing battle. At 12:41 hours Burnett gave the order to cease fire, bringing the second engagement of the day to a close. Burnett decided to use his radar advantage to shadow the *Scharnhorst* from a distance and to wait until Force 2 arrived.

Once again, the *Scharnhorst* performed better than the British cruisers during the exchange of fire, but for the second time that day Konter-Admiral Bey had decided to avoid the fight. Rear Admiral Burnett had successfully protected the convoy, and this time he also maintained contact with the enemy when the engagement drew to a close. Given the superiority of the *Scharnhorst*'s guns and armour, the British ships did well. They had the advantage of taking the enemy by surprise – a benefit provided by radar. During the engagement that followed the *Scharnhorst* was well within visual range, so gunnery solutions could be worked out by observers, just as they were on the German ship. However, despite the close ranges (anything from 6½ down to 2 nautical miles), visibility was hampered slightly by the sleet and snow squalls, which passed between the ships from the south-west, by the smoke from the *Norfolk*'s guns and from hits, and by the rolling, pitching gun platforms themselves. In other words, conditions were far from ideal, and both sides were lucky to score the hits they actually did.

During the battle *Sheffield* fired ninety-six rounds from her main 6-inch guns. For the first seven minutes only her forward turrets could bear, but from 12:28 until 12:41 hours she fired her full broadside of twelve 6-inch guns at the *Scharnhorst*. During the engagement her Type 284 fire control radar was inoperable, which meant that she had to rely on visual observation of her fall of shot, which was used to correct the gunners' aim. However, her type 273 surface search radar was fully operational, and it was found that the set was so accurate that the radar operators could actually detect the fall of shot, thereby providing the gunnery officer with a useful secondary source of information. Finally, her Type 285 fire control radar – used to direct her secondary armament of 4-inch guns – was able to track and hold the target during the engagement, and the information was passed to the men controlling the cruiser's main guns. This situation was repeated on board the *Belfast* and the *Norfolk* – or it was until the heavy cruiser lost her type 273Q radar and her Type 284 fire control radar was damaged. Despite this she still managed to fire her main guns using visual targeting. In all, she fired 161 rounds from her 8-inch guns during the entire day – a total of thirty-one salvos or full broadsides using a mixture of visual and radar-guided fire control.

But on board the *Belfast* all her fire control radar systems were operating at full effectiveness, and were used to correct the aim of her guns. During the whole of 26 December, Burnett's flagship fired thirty-eight broadsides and salvos from her main 6-inch guns – a total of 316 shells. Of these, fourteen broadsides were fired using visual gunnery direction and the rest using radar fire control. Incidentally, the *Belfast* also fired off seventy-seven rounds from her secondary 4-inch guns, whose fire was directed using her Type 285 fire control radar. In other words, the British ships could fire their guns using radar alone, but given the close range of the target they preferred to rely on the older and slightly more reliable method of using observers to direct the aim of their guns. However, they were able to switch to radar-controlled gunnery with relative ease when needed.

On board the *Scharnhorst* Petty Officer Gödde suggested that the British ships had been detected by her Seetakt FuM027 radar. She was fitted with two of these radars, one mounted on her foretop, and the other on top of her after rangefinder. In theory these two sets should have given the *Scharnhorst* an all-round surface search radar capability of around 20 kilometres or 10 nautical miles. These two mattress-shaped antennae were designed to work in conjunction with the 10.5-metre rangefinders fitted beneath them, so that the results from both targeting sources could be compared. The problem was that the surface search radar was unreliable, particularly in poor weather conditions. In reality, the effective range of the radar for gunnery direction purposes was around 10,000 yards (5 nautical miles). That was if everything was fully operational. It was risky to operate, as the British cruisers were equipped with sophisticated passive radar listening equipment and could usually detect German radar transmissions at some considerable distance. But the forward Seetakt radar had been knocked out earlier that morning, during the first clash with the British cruisers. The secondary set mounted towards the stern of the battle-cruiser had a greatly reduced search arc, as the ship itself prevented it from detecting anything ahead of the ship's path. It may also have made the transmission difficult to detect by the British.

If we accept the statement by Petty Officer Gödde, then this meant that the *Scharnhorst* was able to detect the British ships at 12:20 hours, before they could be seen by the lookouts, and just before the star shell from the *Belfast* burst overhead. By this stage the range was down to 11,000 yards (5½ nautical miles). At the time the *Scharnhorst* was heading towards the gap between the British cruisers and the destroyers, but while the destroyers were effectively dead ahead, and therefore out of radar arc, the British cruisers were a little further off the battlecruiser's starboard bow. This put them just on the edge of the radar blind spot caused by the loss of the forward Seetakt radar. This meant that if the *Scharnhorst* did actually detect the leading British cruiser before it opened fire, then her operators were extremely lucky. It might also explain why the *Scharnhorst* was able to return fire so quickly – the basic targeting information was already being passed to her gun crews at 12:21 hours when the star shell was fired. That early warning was about the only piece of luck the so-called 'lucky' ship had during its final day.

It was easy enough to criticise Konter-Admiral Bey with the benefit of hindsight. Grossadmiral Dönitz felt that the Battlegroup commander had somehow lacked the will to fight, ignoring the fact that this was his second attempt to break through to the convoy since dawn. Speaking of the engagement, the German naval commander said:

> This time the *Scharnhorst* was tactically in a much more favourable position, and it was the enemy who were silhouetted against

Day 7: Sunday 26 December 1943

the brighter south-western horizon, while *Scharnhorst* had the dark, northern sector behind her. The correct thing to have done would have been to continue the fight and finish off the weaker British forces, particularly as it was plain they had already been hard hit. If this been done, an excellent opportunity would, of course, have been created.

In fact, Dönitz himself had instructed Bey to break off the attack if he encountered what he deemed a superior force. In his mind Bey was simply following orders. Technically, Force 1 lacked the armour and firepower to match the *Scharnhorst*, but Bey knew that he had lost the tactical initiative, and the longer the battle continued then the worse the odds would become. In these circumstances his decision to break off the attack was understandable.

Another consideration, often overlooked, is that the crew of the *Scharnhorst* had now been battling through a severe gale for more than sixteen hours, and were twelve hours away from the safety of the Altenfjord. Many of her inexperienced crew were seasick, and they had all been at action stations for the past six hours. They had made two attacks against the convoy, and had fought two skirmishes with Force 1. The endurance of the German sailors was being pushed to the limit, and it was inevitable that exhaustion was setting in. Worse still, Bey seemed to be losing faith in his own abilities. After all, on both occasions he had manoeuvred the *Scharnhorst* into an ideal position to attack the convoy, but had run into the enemy covering force instead. On this last brief engagement the British cruisers had managed to deploy directly across his path, as if they knew exactly the direction he planned to attack from, and when he would make his move. Then there was the possibility that another force was lurking out there in the darkness. Given these doubts, and his own lack of luck, it might well have seemed that attempting a third attack on the convoy was beyond the capabilities of ship and crew.

Armchair critics have also managed to find fault in the actions of Rear Admiral Burnett and Commander Fisher. After the battle, an Admiralty report stated that the destroyers should have launched a torpedo assault, despite the poor angle of attack. They ignored the fact that Burnett had ordered the destroyers to make the attack, but the order had never been relayed to Fisher. The critics added that if the four destroyers had been deployed in line abreast, ahead of the cruisers, then they would have been better placed to react to the *Scharnhorst*'s dramatic turn away to the south. The one thing the report did get right was that any destroyer attack would have involved 'getting in close'. The destroyers of the 36th Division were equipped with Mark IX 21-inch torpedoes, carried amidships in two four-torpedo launchers. In theory they had a range of up to 15,000 yards at 35 knots, but in practice a hit was unlikely if the torpedoes were fired at any range over 3,000 yards. To launch a successful attack, Fisher's destroyers would have had to change formation and then close within 1½ nautical miles of the enemy. Even if the order had come through, the chances of success were little better than the chances of survival in the face of the concentrated point-blank firepower of the German battlecruiser.

At 12:40 hours, Bey sent a signal to Narvik and then on to Kiel: 'Square 4133. Engaged by several opponents. Radar-directed fire from heavy units.' This was a bit of a white lie – after all, Kapitän-zur-See Hintze had already announced to the ship's company that the enemy force consisted of three cruisers. During the previous twenty minutes the lookouts on the *Scharnhorst* would have been able to identify the enemy firing at them. It was clear that Bey was simply using the engagement as an excuse to give up the fight. When the message was passed to him, Admiral Schniewind wrote:

> Because of his advanced technology the enemy is able to fight with the aid of radar. *Scharnhorst* has no equivalent equipment. As he is under radar-guided fire by heavy units, in accordance with his orders the Battlegroup commander has broken off the engagement.

This was exactly the vindication that Bey wanted. He was now free to turn for home with a clear conscience.

By 13:00 hours the battle had turned into a chase. The *Scharnhorst* was now powering away to the south-west at 28 knots. From her initial course of 135° she had turned a little more to port, onto a course of 115°, probably in an attempt to shake off her pursuers. By 13:00 hours she came round to 155° (south-south-east), a course that would take her directly back to the Altenfjord. Rear Admiral Burnett

Day 7: Sunday 26 December 1943

was content to match the course and speed of the battlecruiser, and to shadow her from a distance. That afternoon the visibility was around 14,000 yards (just under 7 nautical miles), so Burnett ordered his cruisers to lurk just out of visibility range, about 8 miles astern of the battlecruiser. He ordered his other cruisers to form on the bearing of 245° from his flagship, which meant his three cruisers formed a line roughly at right angles to the enemy. As the ships ran south, he and Admiral Fraser exchanged regular signals so that both admirals knew exactly where they were in relation to each other, and to the enemy. Fraser later called Burnett's performance an exemplary piece of shadowing.

Burnett was lucky. The *Scharnhorst* was heading on a course that meant the gale was hitting Force 1 from the starboard beam. The cruisers and even the destroyers following in their wake were able to cope with the rough seas coming from that quarter, and consequently they were able to match the *Scharnhorst*'s speed. Commander Fisher described how his destroyers coped with the conditions:

> We were doing about 30 knots into a heavy sea. Earlier I had told the Rear Admiral (the destroyer commander in Scapa Flow) that my ship, though splendidly armed with three double turrets and powerful machinery, was useless into a head sea as she was like a silk stocking full of tins of bully beef and one couldn't use her without breaking her up. However, on this occasion a few cracked oil tanks would not have been a court martial offence and we slammed into it regardless and found that once one had passed a critical speed of perhaps 18 knots she sailed over it like a speed-boat zip-zipping and leaving no time for falling into the holes. I suppose that is what the constructors had designed her to do, bless them. But the spray was fiercely stinging.

It must have been an exhilarating experience. In fact, at 16:00 hours Burnett had to order Fisher back into position, as his destroyers were beginning to overtake the cruisers.

The course set by Konter-Admiral Bey was one of the few that allowed Force 1 and the 36th Division to keep pace with the *Scharnhorst*. If he had headed towards the south-west, the smaller British ships would have had to sail directly into the storm, and that meant they would be unable to maintain their speed. Burnett himself had estimated his cruisers could manage little more than 16 knots on a south-westerly course, so by changing course, the *Scharnhorst* could have shaken off her pursuers within two hours – by 15:00 hours at the latest. Instead, she continued on to the south-west – a course Admiral Fraser later described as perfect for the British. Bey knew the British cruisers were shadowing him – the *Scharnhorst* would have been able to pick up traces of their frequent radio signals. He must have wondered why Burnett seemed content to keep his distance, and seemingly to allow the *Scharnhorst* to escape back to the Norwegian coast without trying to delay her.

One likely reason why Bey maintained his course was that he now knew Force 2 was somewhere to the south-west. Around 13:30 hours the news of the Luftwaffe sighting of Fraser's force was finally passed to the *Scharnhorst*, although accurate details of its composition, course and speed were never included in the signal. This, combined with the suspicious radio traffic from Force 1, would have alerted Bey to the possibility that a second British warship group was probably heading towards him. A second error of German communications was that, during the afternoon, the radio exchanges between Force 1 and Force 2 were being picked up by German radio direction finders and then reported to German Naval Headquarters at Kiel. If Admiral Schniewind had kept Bey informed of these latest reports then the Battlegroup commander might have realised he was sailing into a trap and reacted accordingly. But he remained on course.

At 13:45 hours Bey sent a signal to Kapitän-zur-See Johannesson, whose last orders were to close with the convoy and attack. The order called off the attack, leaving the five vessels of the 4th Destroyer Flotilla with nothing to do. However, they were still within striking range of the convoy, and a little after 14:00 hours Kapitänleutnant Lübsen in *U-277* sent a radio message to Narvik, reporting that he had regained contact with the convoy. By that time Convoy JW 55B had settled onto a course of 135°, and just half an hour before had almost blundered across the path of the 36th Destroyer Division. As he ran south in pursuit of the *Scharnhorst* and Force 1, Commander Fisher in HMS *Matchless* reported coming across a darkened ship, crossing his bows from right to left. It was one of the merchantmen from the convoy (probably the *Ocean Gypsy*), which had veered off

Day 7: Sunday 26 December 1943

course and was now on her own. Fisher reported the stray to Captain McCoy as he passed, then raced on to the south.

At 14:20 hours Johannesson in *Z-29* finally received the signal ordering him to return to base. As his destroyers had been buffeted by the gale for hours without even sighting the enemy, he was happy to comply. *Z-33* had become detached, but the remaining four destroyers set course for Point Lucie, approximately 260 miles due south. For them, Operation Ostfront was over. The voyage home was uneventful, although at 18:40 hours Johannesson intercepted a signal suggesting that the *Scharnhorst* was in action again, somewhere to the east. An hour later Kapitän-zur-See Peters in Narvik sent Johannesson another signal, ordering him to rendezvous with the battlecruiser, but at 20:13 hours this order was rescinded, and the 4th Destroyer Flotilla was ordered to return to the Altenfjord. The destroyers reached Point Lucie a little after 01:00 hours the following morning, and after threading their way through the protective minefields they entered the protective waters of the fjord. By 10:00 hours they were safely back at anchor, and a few hours later Kapitän-zur-See Holtorf joined them in *Z-33*. The only member of the Battlegroup that remained at sea was the *Scharnhorst*, and as the destroyers came to anchor their crews still had no news of their comrades.

On board the German battlecruiser the hours passed slowly, and the crew grabbed what sleep they could at their action stations. Around 14:30 hours Kapitän-zur-See Hintze announced over the loudspeaker that the operation against the convoy had been broken off and they were returning to port. An hour later, Bey sent a signal to Narvik, reporting his position, course and speed. He also intimated that he expected to arrive at the Altenfjord a little after midnight. Despite the scattering of intelligence reports to the contrary, Bey and the crew of the *Scharnhorst* thought that the fighting lay behind them, and that nothing could prevent them from reaching their base.

The situation on board the *Duke of York* could hardly have been more different. Fraser knew his force had been spotted by the Luftwaffe, but he knew there was now little the *Scharnhorst* could do to escape the trap. The regular reports from Burnett helped assure him the enemy battlecruiser was still continuing on its general course, although at 14:30 hours she altered course to port, onto a new heading of 170°. Fraser had already learned from Burnett that there was no sign of the

The Battle of North Cape

German destroyers, and he rightly concluded that they had been ordered back to port. The *Scharnhorst* was on her own and Fraser was now confident she could be brought to battle and sunk.

Fraser's Fleet Signals Officer, Lieutenant Commander Courage, said of the situation that it was: 'Money for old rope. From here on in it was an execution job.' If Fraser lacked the conviction of his subordinates, he succeeded in hiding his nerves. Lieutenant Cox of the admiral's staff recalled that during the afternoon Admiral Fraser seemed in his element:

> He wore no naval uniform, as such, he just wore old trousers and a polo neck shirt, polo neck sweater and a rather battered admiral's hat and with his pipe belching sparks and flame. He moved amongst us all, being extremely confident and quiet and delightful … It was a real triumph of a single personality dominating a ship's company.

The only real changes to the situation as the afternoon wore on were technical rather than strategic. At 13:47 hours Captain Bain in the *Norfolk* reported that his Type 273Q search radar was now operational again, which meant that, despite the hits she had suffered, she was now fully operational – albeit her firepower had been cut by a quarter to just six 8-inch guns. Given the concerns about her damage it was a real feat that she managed to maintain her place with the rest of Force 2, as Burnett's cruisers continued to shadow the enemy.

After studying the plot Fraser was now engaged in a little morale boosting. As he recalled in his diary: 'We wondered whether we should have the battle before tea or after tea. We decided we should have it after tea.' This might have been a battle fought in near total darkness and in the teeth of a gale, but at least the Royal Navy were trying to keep up standards. Consequently, at 14:17 hours, Fraser sent a signal to all ships:

> If enemy maintains present course and speed, action should be joined at 16:30 hours.' Now everyone knew what to expect, and when. As Lieutenant Commander Courage put it: 'that was a nice little signal. There was the C-in-C puffing away at his pipe, though he was still outside, still on the outer bridge.… Here he was,

Day 7: Sunday 26 December 1943

telling the world in general what was happening, saying he hoped to be there at 16:30 hours. Mark you, there were a couple of hours to go. We were having a happy time in *Duke of York*.

At 15:15 hours Admiral Fraser made another signal, this time to inform the rest of Force 2 that the estimated course and bearing of the enemy from the flagship was now 025°, and 56 nautical miles away. This meant that, at present course and speed, Fraser's force would go into action almost exactly the time that Fraser had predicted earlier, in a little over an hour. Everyone knew that battle was imminent – or at least everyone on the British ships did. On board the *Scharnhorst* there was no inkling the battle was about to reach its bloody conclusion. Almost half an hour later, at 15:42 hours, Fraser ordered another signal to be sent to the rest of Force 2: 'Observe very attentively Admiral's motions as he will probably alter his course or speed, either with or without signal, as may be most convenient.' It was a standard form of wording, implying that anything could happen when the battle started, and that all captains should be ready.

So far Fraser had done everything he could to bring the *Scharnhorst* to bay. So far everything had gone according to plan. But in the final minutes before the battle things started to go badly wrong. The first piece of bad news came at 15:45 hours, when Captain Bain reported that a fire had re-ignited in a wing compartment over one of the *Norfolk*'s main oil fuel tanks. The only way to fight the fire was to stop the ship from rolling so badly, which meant pulling out of the chase. Consequently, the *Norfolk* turned to port onto a north-easterly heading, in order to present her stern to the gale. Until she dealt with the problem she would take no further part in the coming battle. Fortunately, Captain Bain's damage control teams were extremely efficient and the heavy cruiser was able to rejoin the battle by 17:00 hours.

A few minutes later, at 16:10 hours, a second of Rear Admiral Burnett's cruisers was forced to abandon the pursuit. Captain Addis of the *Sheffield* reported that his cruiser had stripped the gearing in her main port turbine, and the inner port propeller shaft had to be stopped. That meant the speed of the light cruiser was now reduced to just 8 knots. Captain Addis's engineers managed to repair the gearing with commendable alacrity, but by reducing her speed the *Sheffield* had dropped behind in the chase. At 16:20 she was able to increase speed to 23 knots, but by that time the gap between her and the *Scharnhorst* had widened and the British cruiser was never able to make up her lost time. As Admiral Fraser put it: 'For the rest of the action she remained some 10 miles astern, conforming to the general movement of the battle.' Consequently, she would play no part in the fighting which followed – a bitter blow to Captain Addis and his crew.

The temporary loss of the *Norfolk* and the *Sheffield* created a potentially dangerous situation for Rear Admiral Burnett. Within a few minutes Force 1 lost two of its three cruisers, leaving the *Belfast* and Fisher's four destroyers on their own. If the *Scharnhorst* had doubled back to the north the *Belfast* would have been in serious trouble. Fortunately, the unsuspecting German battlecruiser remained on course. Captain Parham of the *Belfast* recalled: 'We were alone, shadowing that great ship. She was much bigger than us. She'd only got to turn around for ten minutes and she could have blown us clean out of the water.' Force 1 might have been seriously weakened just minutes before battle was joined, but at least Fraser and Burnett still had one crucial advantage of their opponent. They still had the element of surprise on their side.

The Dog Watches (16:00–19:59 hours)

Just like the previous two clashes, this third and final encounter with the *Scharnhorst* would be a battle where radar proved to be the key. The flagship was certainly well-equipped for the job: it was widely held that in late 1943 the *Duke of York* had the best radar equipment of any warship in the Royal Navy. The main surface search set – the Type 273Q – was mounted on top of the forward gunnery control tower, and had a range of approximately 20 nautical miles, although detection at 23 miles was possible with large contacts like the *Scharnhorst*. The 'Q' designation meant that it was an improvement on the older version of the radar, with a stabilising mechanism that improved performance in rough seas – just like the ones the *Duke of York* was sailing through. Although her Type 281 set was primarily designed for the detection of aircraft, it had a useful surface capability too, with a theoretical range of 12 nautical miles, although after some fine-tuning results had recently been achieved at ranges of 23 miles.

Day 7: Sunday 26 December 1943

In extremis, these two radar systems could be used to direct the ship's guns, although they weren't really designed as fire control radars. For that the *Duke of York* had its own dedicated sets, the Type 284 (Mark III) which served her main 14-inch guns, and the Type 285 (Mark III), which directed the fire of the battleship's 5.25-inch guns. In fact the *Duke of York* carried several sets of these – two Type 284 radars (one mounted forward on top of the visual 14-inch gun director, the other aft), and no less than four Type 285 sets, two to port (labelled Penzance and Paignton), and two to starboard (Saltash and Stonehouse). As well as all these radars, the battleship was also fitted with an extensive suite of electronic equipment, designed to detect aircraft radio or radar transmissions, IFF (Identification of Friend or Foe) transmissions from friendly aircraft or ships, and radar detection equipment. The battleship was buzzing with electronics, and although these were fairly rudimentary by modern standards, in late 1943 they were 'state-of-the-art', and that afternoon they were all working perfectly. Better still, thanks to Fraser's intervention, all the radar operators had just enjoyed a steaming mug of tea and were ready for anything.

During this time Force 2 was steering a course of 080° at 25 knots, an uncomfortable speed for the battleship, which had a tendency to plunge into the waves rather than ride over them when the wind and waves were on her starboard quarter. It was worse for the men in the accompanying destroyers (*Savage*, *Saumarez*, *Scorpion* and *Stord*), although not impossible, while the *Jamaica* fared better than the rest.

Admiral Fraser had confidently predicted that the radar operators on board the *Duke of York* would pick up the 'jig' of the *Scharnhorst* at 16:15 hours. For once Fraser got it wrong. The *Scharnhorst* was detected two minutes later than he had predicted, at 16:17 hours. Given the conditions and the radar technology this was something of a miracle in itself, but then the radar operators were well trained, and had been expecting to make contact. The 'jig' was detected at maximum range for the Type 273Q set – 46,000 yards (23 nautical miles), on a bearing of 020°, which put the *Scharnhorst* to the north-north-east of Fraser's force. After tracking her for several minutes the information supplied by *Belfast* was confirmed – Force 2 and the German battlecruiser were on converging courses.

The Battle of North Cape

Fraser decided not to deviate from his plan, and Force 2 maintained its current course and speed. Seven minutes after making contact the range had decreased to 20 nautical miles, and by 16:36 hours it had reduced to 26,000 yards (13 nautical miles). Seven minutes after that it was down to just 16,000 yards, or 8 nautical miles. All this time the admiral held fire, saying to his staff: 'While the enemy doesn't know we're there, the closer we get, the more certain we'll be.' Since he first plotted the interception, Fraser had planned to open fire at 13,000 yards (6½ nautical miles). He would then launch his destroyers in a torpedo attack. At that range the battleship's secondary armament of 5.25-inch guns could have some effect, as could the 6-inch guns of the *Jamaica*. Of course it was a risk – at that range the 11-inch guns of the *Scharnhorst* could easily cause a devastating penetrating hit on the battleship or the light cruiser, or blow one of the destroyers completely out of the water.

The only change Fraser made to his dispositions during this final approach to battle was to split his destroyers into two sub-divisions, with *Savage* and *Saumarez* off the port bow of the battleship, and *Scorpion* and *Stord* off the starboard bow. The *Jamaica* followed in line astern of the *Duke of York*. The officers of the cruiser had already dubbed their ship 'Little Miss Echo', seeing themselves as little more than the shadow of the battleship. However, Fraser's shortening of the range had largely been for the benefit of the *Jamaica*'s guns. Finally, at 16:37 hours, Fraser signalled to his destroyers: 'Take up most advantageous position for firing torpedoes but do not attack until ordered.'

Everyone in Force 2 knew that within minutes they would not only sight the enemy, but would be launched into battle against one of the most powerful ships in the German Navy. Lieutenant Ramsden of the Royal Marines was manning the after gunnery director on board the *Jamaica*, and therefore had a perfect viewpoint from which to watch the battle unfold. He spoke of the moments before the battle started:

At about four o'clock, the order came through – 'Look out bearing Red Five Oh.' That gave the approximate bearing of the enemy when it appeared. I strained my eyes through the binocular sight, and saw nothing save a black empty horizon.

Day 7: Sunday 26 December 1943

At 16:37 hours the *Duke of York* and the *Belfast* picked each other up on radar at a range of 40,000 yards (20 nautical miles), meaning that Admiral Fraser and Rear Admiral Burnett had effectively now joined forces. The British were closing for the kill.

By this stage, Konter-Admiral Bey apparently knew he was in danger. According to *Scharnhorst* survivor Petty Officer Gödde:

> At about 15:45 hours we were again placed at readiness for instant action. At 16:00 hours the alarm sounded. The Captain himself came in on the gunnery phone, and said something to the effect that we were not out of danger, and exhorted us to keep a sharp lookout. 'You know that ever since midday we've had a pursuer astern who we've not been able to shake off, and our radar tells us that there are more targets to starboard. Keep alert; we shall soon be in the thick of things again.'

For the tired, seasick crew – who just wanted to get back to port safely – this was hardly good news. As there is no evidence that the *Scharnhorst* had her radar switched on, it seems far more likely that she had just detected enemy radar transmissions using her passive electronic detection equipment. Besides, at that stage both Force 1 and Force 2 were beyond the range of her one operational FuMo 27 radar set. The reference to an enemy force to starboard is revealing, and suggests that the *Scharnhorst* had already detected Force 2 before it came into radar range. However, in several other cases the timing of Petty Officer Gödde's testimony suggests that on occasion his recollection was shaky. Certainly a signal sent by Bey to Kapitän-zur-See Peters in Narvik at 16:30 hours makes no mention of detecting Force 2, but merely implies that the crew of the *Scharnhorst* knew they were being shadowed by Force 1: 'Shadower (naval) keeping pace. My position AC4595.'

At 16:42 hours the *Scharnhorst* was seen to change course slightly to port, possibly in a vain attempt to shake off the pursuing cruisers of Force 1. This forced the British to hurriedly recalculate the relative positions of their ships to the *Scharnhorst*, and to feed the new bearing and range information to the gunnery control centres. She was now on a heading of 140°. This forced Fraser to alter course slightly to starboard, in order to widen his 'A-arcs'. That was the angle at which a ship could fire all its main gun turrets. In the case of the *Duke of York* and the *Jamaica*, this meant turning slightly so that the rear turrets of the two ships could bear on the target, which was now 13,000 yards away (6½ nautical miles). Minutes later Fraser ordered *Belfast* to open fire with a star shell, which she did at 16:47 hours. For some reason it failed to illuminate the target, so the *Duke of York* fired four star shell rounds from her port 5.25-inch battery. This time the star shells burst directly over the German battlecruiser, and the *Scharnhorst* was suddenly bathed in light.

Observers in Force 2 saw the enemy lit up like she was a recognition model. It was a magnificent sight. Lieutenant Ramsden in the *Jamaica* remembered her as: 'A black silhouette against the flickering candle-glow. Even at that distance the sheer of her bows was perfectly notice-able and she stood out clearly for an instant as if removed bodily from her page in *Jane's Fighting Ships*.' On the *Duke of York*, Admiral Fraser described the moment he finally saw the ship he had spent a week stalking: 'Four star shells and there she was. . . . It was terrific – I can still see that illumination now.' What was even more astounding was that it was immediately obvious that the *Scharnhorst*'s crew had been taken completely by surprise. Her gun turrets were still trained fore and aft.

Then the *Duke of York* fired her first salvo. Four seemingly endless minutes had passed between the illumination of the *Scharnhorst* and the order to fire, but the British were now wise to the *Scharnhorst*, and knew she would respond with an immediate course change to throw off the inevitable first salvo. Fraser simply waited to see what the target would do before giving the order to open fire. However, for once, Kapitän-zur-See Hintze seemed unprepared, probably – as has been suggested – that he and the Konter-Admiral were off the bridge when the star shells burst. This time the battlecruiser remained on her present course for eight long minutes after being illuminated, until Hintze finally turned his ship hard to port at 16:55 hours. That was four minutes after the British battleship opened fire, and by that time the *Scharnhorst* was already in trouble. For the *Duke of York*'s Gunnery Officer, Lieutenant Commander Crawford, 'It was a gunnery officer's dream come true.' He remembered what he experienced just

Day 7: Sunday 26 December 1943

before the order came to open fire: 'To see this incredible sight about 7 or 8 miles away, like a great silver ghost coming at you ...'

Magnificent though the *Scharnhorst* was, she was also a target. When the order came at 16:51 hours the range was down to 11,950 yards (5½ nautical miles). As soon as the order to open fire was given the *Duke of York* raised two enormous battle ensigns to its mastheads. This was going to be an old-fashioned fight, fought in a time-honoured way. Crawford described firing the first salvo:

> She was 12,000 yards off and showed up well, the first impression being her huge length. The chief thing that remains in my mind was the red glow of the 'Gun Ready' lamps. Suddenly there was a yell of 'Target!' and someone shouted 'There she is plain as a bloody pikestaff!' The Captain said 'Open fire' and I ordered 'Shoot!' Ding-dong went the fire gongs and then there was the agonising wait of three seconds and then the crash as our ten 14-inch gun broadside thundered out. We counted to fifteen and down they came. The splashes completely obliterated *Scharnhorst*, and then there followed a greenish glow along her waterline where she had been hit.

On board the *Scharnhorst*, Gunner Backhaus was manning one of the forward 105mm (4.1-inch guns) on the battlecruiser's superstructure, and so had an excellent view of the scene:

> I was standing on the platform, as I had been pretty well ever since we left the Langefjord. Suddenly there were flashes of light to the south-west and north. We were bathed in light – it was like midday. Enormous spouts of water rose on both sides, unpleasantly close. They towered above me – I was drenched in spray!

Another problem caused by the star shells was that they temporarily blinded the German lookouts, and therefore made it impossible to visually acquire the enemy targets until they extinguished themselves. To hurry that along, the battlecruiser's anti-aircraft guns (20mm and 37mm weapons) were ordered to try to shoot them down. On his

The Battle of North Cape

searchlight platform by the bridge, Petty Officer Gödde recalled that: 'the first star shells were hanging over the ship, and before long heavy shells were whining their way towards us.'

It was an extremely accurate first salvo. The target was straddled, and one shell landed on the starboard side of the battlecruiser's forward turret 'Anton', putting it out of action. Green sparks were seen as shells struck the enemy hull. The ease with which the 14-inch shell had penetrated the heavily armoured turret of the *Scharnhorst* demonstrated just how close the range was. Gödde recalled that:

> 'Anton' turret was jammed facing starboard, and could no longer be rotated. Later I heard on the guns phone that there was no sign of life in the turret. Because of the fire and dense smoke it could no longer take part in the battle.

Gunner (Matrosengefreiter) Rudi Birke in 'Bruno' turret added that a fire broke out, which threatened to spread to the turret's magazine. To prevent an explosion the crew immediately flooded part of their forward magazine:

> We struggled about in the icy water and tried to save as much of the ammunition as possible. A few critical minutes passed before the water was pumped out and 'Bruno' turret was rendered serviceable again.

Jamaica opened fire a minute after the *Duke of York*, and Lieutenant Ramsden recalled the moment:

> The concussion momentarily deafened me, and my vision was blurred by the shaking of the director and the sudden flash out of the gloom. We could see the tracer shells coursing away like a swarm of bees bunched together, and could follow them as they curved gently down towards the target. Before they landed the guns spoke again, and the sea was lighted for a brief second by the livid flash.

The *Jamaica* straddled the *Scharnhorst* with her third salvo, scoring at least one hit.

Day 7: Sunday 26 December 1943

Ramsden also described the effect of witnessing the *Duke of York*'s fire:

> Then the *Duke of York* fired her 14-inch (again), and even to us, now a thousand yards astern, the noise and concussion was colossal, and the vivid spurt of flame lighted up the whole ship for an instant, leaving a great drift of cordite smoke hanging in the air. Her tracers rose quickly, and, in a bunch, sailed up to the highest point of their trajectory, and then curved down, down towards the target.

A shell from the *Duke of York*'s third salvo hit the after superstructure of the *Scharnhorst* forward of 'Caesar' turret and after gunnery control tower, demolishing the battlecruiser's seaplane hangar and causing extensive damage to her after superstructure. Helmut Backhaus, manning one of the forward 105mm (4.1-inch guns), said of the hit:

> The anti-aircraft crews were sent to put it out. There was aircraft fuel in the hangar, and the heat was overpowering. It looked very dangerous until we got it under control.

Several men were killed before the blaze was extinguished. By that time the *Scharnhorst* had finally swung away to port, and was settling onto a northerly course – approximately 010°. The situation after the first ten minutes of battle was that the *Scharnhorst* was now heading north, at full speed. Some 9 nautical miles to the north lay Force 1, with *Belfast* leading *Norfolk* on a south-south-easterly course. The *Sheffield* still lagged some way behind. To the west of the *Belfast* were the four destroyers of Commander Fisher's 36th Destroyer Division. Six miles to the south the *Duke of York*, followed by the *Jamaica*, were firing with deadly accuracy, while heading east. On either side of the battleship were two destroyers (*Savage* and *Saumarez*) to the north and *Scorpion* and *Stord* to the south. The only chance of escape for the *Scharnhorst* lay to the east.

After the third salvo from the *Duke of York* smoke was pouring from the German battlecruiser's forward turret and her after super-structure, and she no longer looked the sleek beautiful ship she had appeared just minutes earlier. A side effect of the hit on her after superstructure was that the explosion killed or wounded several of the crews of her exposed 20mm and 37mm anti-aircraft guns – the very men who had been firing at the star shells just moments before. As a result the remaining crews were ordered to take shelter below decks, as were the gun crews of the seven twin 105mm (4.1-inch) turrets, which lacked the armoured protection afforded to the ship's heavier armament. This meant that, at a stroke, the *Scharnhorst* had lost her best weapon against enemy destroyers – just at the moment when Admiral Fraser's four 'S' class destroyers were approaching the battlecruiser from the south-west. But before the battlecruiser made her turn to the north, and just six minutes after being taken by surprise by the star shells, the *Scharnhorst* opened fire with her main guns, directing her first salvo at the *Duke of York*.

Her first salvo, fired at 16:53 hours, comprised just six 11-inch shells, as by that stage 'Anton' turret was already out of action. 'Bruno' and 'Caesar' turrets fired to starboard using visual direction – the FuMo radar appears to have been switched off when the battle started, probably to reduce the risk of detection by enemy electronic surveillance equipment. Her first salvo fell well short of the British battleship, but her shooting soon improved, and by her third salvo she was straddling the target. On the bridge of the *Duke of York* Lieutenant Commander Courage had no official task, so all he could do was stand on the bridge wing where he 'could see nothing except the splashing of *Scharnhorst*'s shells, which seemed to be much too close for comfort'. To aid her gunnery the *Scharnhorst* also fired star shells from her starboard 150mm (5.9-inch) guns, which burst between the *Duke of York* and the *Jamaica*. Like the 8-inch guns of the *Norfolk*, the 5.25-inch secondary guns of the *Duke of York* didn't use flashless cordite, which meant that, when they fired, they were highly visible to German observers. Lieutenant Ramsden on board *Jamaica* described the experience of being illuminated:

> From that distance the firing of these was quite invisible until the shells burst, two or three together, with intense white flares which hung in the air above us. In their light the sea was lit up as by the moon very brightly, and I remember thinking that we must have

Day 7: Sunday 26 December 1943

been visible for miles. I felt as if I had been stripped stark naked, and had to resist the natural urge to hide behind something away from the light, as if it would have mattered!

Then came the enemy salvo:

Just as we had again been plunged into the comforting gloom I saw the angry white wink of her first 11-inch broadside, and said to myself, 'She's fired' [...] Thank God we couldn't see her shells coming as we could see ours going. The waiting for their arrival was bad enough, but to see them coming all the way would have been far more grim. There was a vague flash off the port bow which I caught in the corner of my eye as I gazed through the binoculars, and then – crack, crack, crack, sharp like a giant whip, and the drone and whine of splinters passing somewhere near.

On the *Duke of York* and the *Jamaica* the radar operators were able to track the course of the shells as they flew towards them.

The turn to the north at 16:55 hours simply brought the *Scharnhorst* closer to the ships of Force 1. Gunner Backhaus described the situation with unusual clarity: 'It was a terrifying sight. We were under fire from every direction. We seemed to be surrounded by enemy ships.' A minute later, at 16:56, Konter-Admiral Bey sent a signal to Kiel, forwarded through Narvik. It read: 'Square AC4677. Heavy battleship – am in action.' It was something of an understatement, as, although the *Scharnhorst* had turned away from Fraser's Force 2, it was still heading directly towards Burnett's Force 1. At that moment *Belfast* opened fire, as did the *Norfolk*, which had steamed at full speed to catch up with Burnett's flagship after falling behind to put out a fire. The firing of the *Norfolk*'s 8-inch guns, using 'full-flash' propellant, took Burnett and his staff by surprise – they had been so intent on the spectacle of the *Scharnhorst* turning towards them that they hadn't noticed the *Norfolk* coming up astern of them. On board the *Scharnhorst* the secondary gunnery teams briefly switched their attention to Burnett's cruisers, which at that moment represented almost as much of a threat as the *Duke of York*.

The Battle of North Cape

When *Scharnhorst* began her initial turn to the north at 16:55 hours, a brief alarm was felt on board the *Duke of York*, as it was feared she might have fired a spread of torpedoes towards the British battleship. Possibly someone saw splashes from shellfire, which they imagined were torpedoes hitting the water. As a precaution Captain Parham of the *Duke of York* ordered his ship to steer 060°, in effect heading directly towards the torpedo threat. This meant 'combing' the torpedo tracks – trying to steer between the torpedoes coming towards him, while making his own ship as hard to hit as possible. The *Scharnhorst* was never designed to carry torpedoes, but in 1941 two three-torpedo launchers were removed from the light cruiser *Nurnberg*, and fitted to the deck of the battlecruiser (one launcher on either side of her superstructure) just astern of the funnel. The report proved groundless, and the battleship soon swung back to her original course, with the *Jamaica* following in her wake.

At 17:00 hours – or just after – the *Scharnhorst* was hit again. Shortly after she began her turn to the south-east. Ordinary Seaman (Matrosengefreiter) Günther Sträter, manning one of the after 105mm (4.1-inch) guns, felt the ship buck beneath him:

> I supposed we had been hit amidships, perhaps on the port side
> ... the commander of the gun crew, Wibbelhoff, ordered us to
> put on our gas masks.

Smoke and acrid fumes would have been lingering around these exposed gun positions, making it hard for the crews to follow orders and reach safety below decks. Despite the damage to her armament and superstructure her engines were still working perfectly, and at this stage of the battle she was probably steaming at her maximum speed – around 30 knots.

At 17:08 hours Hintze gave the only sensible order in the circumstances, and the *Scharnhorst* altered course to the east, heading away from the two enemy forces on a heading of 111°. By then her turn to the north had meant that the *Scharnhorst* had increased the gap between her and the *Duke of York* to 17,000 yards (8½ nautical miles).

Fraser ordered the *Duke of York* and *Jamaica* to turn to starboard onto a parallel course, which put Force 2 on the starboard beam of

Day 7: Sunday 26 December 1943

the German battlecruiser. While the *Scharnhorst* completed her turn 'Caesar' turret continued to fire, supported when her 'A arc' was opened by 'Bruno' turret. So far Bey and Hintze had reacted well, and despite the damage meted out by the *Duke of York*'s 14-inch guns, they were fighting their ship with commendable skill. However, around 17:05 hours, a salvo from the battleship hit the *Scharnhorst* just forward of her bridge, and a 14-inch shell pierced the ventilation trunking of 'Bruno' turret, temporarily rendering it inoperable. That meant that only 'Caesar' turret was still able to retaliate. But its gunners were fighting back. Wing Commander Compston, attached to Fraser's staff, was watching the battle from the *Duke of York*'s bridge:

> On our port bow we saw the flashes from the guns of the cruiser *Belfast* as she engaged the enemy yet again that day, while the brilliant flash of the *Scharnhorst*'s guns, firing broadsides at the flagship enabled us to mark her position in the darkness [...] During this amazing fireworks display the officers on the bridge were calmly going about their duties, sending vital signals and even finding time in between our broadsides and those of the enemy to give their men a running commentary on events over the loudspeaker. Star shells from both sides lit up the scene continuously. It is curious how naked one feels when a very bright light descends in one's vicinity – 'now we shall catch it' is the feeling.

The *Duke of York* was extremely lucky during this duel with the *Scharnhorst* – the only damage she sustained came when two 11-inch shells struck the battleship's foremast. According to Compston:

> A sudden rattle of bits and pieces falling proved, on examination after the battle, that an eleven inch shell had severed rope and steel stays on the foremast just abaft the bridge.

In fact the shells had passed through the mast, destroying the aerial of the Type 281 air warning set, and damaging the Type 273 surface search radar. Fortunately, Lieutenant Bates and two ratings were on hand in the radar shack, mounted on the mast just above where the shells had hit. As he put it, when the shells struck:

> The shock was terrific and the three occupants collapsed in a heap on the very small deck. To their amazement, they were not injured at all and moreover the radar set appeared to be working. But there was no echo now from the *Scharnhorst*.

Clearly there was something wrong with the surface search radar. Bates traced the problem to a severed electrical cable, leading up to the aerial from his own radar shack:

> I switched off the 'office' lights and climbed up into the aerial compartment. By feeling about and aided by letting a pocket torch peep between my fingers, I found the aerials pointing to the sky. By operating the appropriate controls, I got the aerials horizontal and stabilised again by their gyroscope and the sea echoes and echo of *Scharnhorst* were restored. So it was the horrific shock of the German 11-inch shell passing through the mast that had made the aerials topple over. Fortunately all the electrical wires to the set passed along the fore front of the mast and so did not get damaged.

When he repaired the connection Bates became something of a naval legend. By the time the tale was retold by the rest of the battleship's crew, Bates – a tall, burly officer – had held the damaged wires together by brute strength, and had respliced them using his bare hands. Henceforth he was known as 'Barehand Bates'. The tale was later picked up by the British press, who managed to garble the story even more, as radar was still considered a 'top secret' invention. As the novelist C.S. Forester wrote:

> Bates effected a temporary repair in the quickest possible way. He climbed the mast – in the dark, with the wind whipping round him and the ship lurching fantastically over the waves – and he held the ends of the aerial together for the orders to pass.

Although the truth was less dramatic, it meant that, apart from the Type 281 set, which was damaged beyond repair, the *Duke of York*

Day 7: Sunday 26 December 1943

was still able to engage the enemy using her full suite of detection and fire control radars.

When Force 2 altered course towards the north-east at 16:55 hours during the torpedo scare, the destroyers accompanying the two larger warships continued on their original course, and they were now coming so close to the *Scharnhorst* that the most northerly of the four – *Savage* and *Saumarez* – were being illuminated by the star shells, which were still being fired by the *Duke of York*'s 5.25-inch guns, and which were bursting over the enemy battlecruiser. In fact, at 17:00 hours, HMS *Savage* actually turned away from the enemy, steaming in a full circle to avoid coming so close to her that British shells could hit this destroyer rather than the *Scharnhorst*.

All of the destroyer commanders were waiting for one order: to attack with torpedoes. Fraser's reluctance to release the destroyers was based on his understanding that, in those sea conditions, it would be impossible to reload the tubes. Rather than risk an unplanned attack he considered it much more prudent to wait until the enemy had been damaged sufficiently to reduce her ability to manoeuvre. Then she would be unable to avoid the torpedoes, and the 'one-shot weapon' would not be wasted. Consequently, Admiral Fraser still stood by his original order: 'Do not attack until ordered.'

But by 17:13 hours the situation had changed. It had become apparent that, after turning onto her new south-easterly course, the *Scharnhorst* was pulling away from her pursuers. Fraser decided to send in the destroyers. Fraser therefore repeated the signal, 'take up the most advantageous position for torpedo attack', but then added 'close and attack with torpedoes'. In theory this meant that Commander Meyrick and his four destroyers would move onto the beam of the enemy battlecruiser, ready to launch their torpedoes when ordered. But by that stage it had become impossible for Meyrick to comply. *Savage* and *Saumarez* were now to the west of the *Scharnhorst*, and were unable to match the battlecruiser's speed through the rough seas. There was no way they could overhaul her. The effective range of a 21-inch Mark IX torpedo in those sea conditions was less than 2,000 yards – just 1 nautical mile. The only way Meyrick could reach his firing position was if the *Scharnhorst* could be slowed down.

Scorpion and *Stord* were trying the same thing a little to the south and east, and although they were better placed to intercept the *Scharnhorst*, conditions were far from favourable. As Lieutenant Commander Storheill, the Norwegian skipper of the *Stord* put it:

> The sea was very rough – it was like surfing – and on the *Stord* and other destroyers we were prepared for the same surprises that are a part of that sport.

In other words the destroyers were in grave danger of being pushed beam on to the waves and capsizing in the rough seas. Despite their best efforts the destroyer captains found themselves unable to work their way any closer to the *Scharnhorst*. Still, although the *Scharnhorst* was now drawing well away from the *Belfast* and *Norfolk*, the *Duke of York* and the *Jamaica* were still scoring hits. On board the *Scharnhorst* Gunner Sträter learned of another hit at around 17:15 hours:

> The first 15cm. gun crew on the starboard side reported that a shell had penetrated their magazine and the gun was out of action. The men in the magazine were killed outright. The survivors were told to make their way forward to their assembly point.

This hit also penetrated the armoured belt on the ship's port side, abreast of the bridge, just above the waterline. A damage control party raced to plug the hole, and a patch was soon welded in position.

The danger of an explosion was bad enough, but any fire also made the job of enemy fire control even easier, as it made the burning target highly visible in the darkness. Fortunately for the *Scharnhorst* her crew managed to extinguish the fire in the hangar by that stage, and as the range between the British battleship and German battle-cruiser had now extended to 12,500 yards (just over 6 nautical miles), visual spotting was becoming increasingly difficult. Consequently, at 17:17 hours, the *Duke of York* was forced to rely solely on radar fire control. As for the *Scharnhorst*, she had to rely on spotting the enemy muzzle flashes, described as 'great deep orange flashes in the Arctic darkness'. At 17:24 hours Bey sent another understated signal: 'Am surrounded by heavy units.' Again, this was not strictly true. By that stage it appeared that he and Hintze had managed to wriggle their way out of Admiral Fraser's trap.

Day 7: Sunday 26 December 1943

By now it was becoming apparent to Generaladmiral Schniewind in Kiel that a failed operation was now on the brink of becoming a disaster. First was the signal sent by Bey at 16:30 hours, informing him that the *Scharnhorst* was still being shadowed, presumably by enemy cruisers. Then came the signal at 16:56 hours – less than thirty minutes later – which read: 'Heavy battleship – am in action.' Finally, less than thirty minutes after that, came the third signal: 'Am surrounded by heavy units.' It didn't take a tactical genius to work out what had happened. First, the cruiser force protecting the convoy had followed the *Scharnhorst* as it steamed southwards towards the Norwegian coast. That was almost certainly the shadowing force Bey mentioned first. Then there was the battleship. For the past two days, signals had been intercepted suggesting there might well be a naval force operating in the Barents Sea, somewhere to the south of the convoy. Signals between two forces had been detected during the afternoon. Then there was the Luftwaffe sighting of that force earlier that morning, in the vicinity of North Cape. It was clear by now that this was a second covering force, and that it contained a battleship with the firepower to match that of the *Scharnhorst*. Bey was clearly in a difficult situation.

Bey's second signal, at 16:30, was intercepted by Kapitän-zur-See Johannesson in *Z-29*, which at that stage was well to the west, heading back towards the Altenfjord. It was clear neither Schniewind nor Peters had any real idea what was happening, or where Johannesson's 4th Destroyer Flotilla was in relation to the *Scharnhorst*. When he intercepted the signal, a despairing Johannesson wrote in his diary:

> This report is very disturbing. Either the Northern Group has caught up with the *Scharnhorst*, or thanks to the bearings, a Southern Group has reached her. [Following the interception of the next signal, Johannesson added] I am afraid that the fate of the ship is sealed.

However, Johannesson was not prepared to abandon the battlecruiser to her fate. He ordered his destroyers to alter course to the east, in the hope that he might be able to do something to alter the outcome of the battle.

The Battle of North Cape

At 18:15 hours Kapitän-zur-See Peters sent Johannesson official orders to intervene. The destroyer commander had just written in his diary:

> Whether it is possible to help the *Scharnhorst* in what is obviously an unequal battle is impossible to say. No order has reached this flotilla, but this calls for action.

For a flotilla commander who had blithely followed orders all day, this was a refreshing display of initiative, and the orders from Narvik must have eased Johannesson's doubts that he was making the right decision. At the same time, Peters sent an identical signal to the U-boats of Gruppe Eisenbart, ordering them to 'Steer at top speed to AC4930.' Unfortunately for Konter-Admiral Bey, these orders came too late.

Meanwhile, the *Scharnhorst* continued to outpace the British ships. At 17:42 hours the *Jamaica* ceased fire, as the range had now increased to 18,000 yards (9 nautical miles), which was beyond the effective range of her 6-inch guns. In the past fifty minutes she had fired sixteen full broadsides, and had scored at least one confirmed hit. As Lieutenant Ramsden put it:

> After a little the range increased, which rendered our 6-inch rather out of it, and that, combined with the fact that our shell splashes might have confused the flagship's spotting, made us cease fire temporarily, and we could follow the battle more closely.

Commander Meyrick's four destroyers were now more than 12,000 yards (6 nautical miles) away from the *Scharnhorst*, and falling further behind every minute. The cruisers of Force 1 were even further behind – the *Belfast* and *Norfolk* were now well to the west of the *Scharnhorst*, with the *Sheffield* lagging behind the rest of the force. At 17:15 hours Burnett had ordered his ships to cease fire, and five minutes later he signalled Fraser to report that he had lost touch with his quarry. Still, the cruisers of Force 1 continued to pursue the *Scharnhorst* as best they could, hoping for some kind of miracle.

When the *Jamaica* ceased fire the only ships left in the fight were the *Scharnhorst* and the *Duke of York*. At that point the *Duke of York*

Day 7: Sunday 26 December 1943

was just ahead of *Jamaica*, and 17,000 yards (8½ nautical miles) from the *Scharnhorst*. Her 14-inch guns were still well within range – in theory they had a maximum effective range using radar fire control of 29,000 yards (or just under 15 nautical miles). But the angle to the target meant that the battleship could barely clear her 'A arcs' – her stern turret was trained forward on its extreme bearing, and at that angle accurate fire control was hindered far more than normal by the movement of the ship. That meant her maximum effective range in these sea conditions was reduced to about 21,000 yards (10½ nautical miles). By that stage the damage to 'Bruno' turret had been repaired, and so Hintze was able to fire steadily with 'Caesar' turret, and then from time to time he would yaw his ship slightly until he cleared his own 'A arc', allowing 'Bruno' turret to add her weight to the salvo. At that range any hits by either ship would be a matter of sheer luck. On the *Jamaica*, Lieutenant Ramsden was able to follow the battle more closely after his ship had stopped firing:

It was a slogging match between giants, appalling in their might and fury. Every time the *Duke of York* fired there came the vivid flicker of the *Scharnhorst*'s reply, the lazy flight of the 14-inch tracer followed by the crack, crack, of the 11-inch reply in the sea, and the drone of splinters. At one period we were engaged fine on our port bow, and both sides fired a succession of star shells for the greater accuracy of their main armament. I suddenly remembered my camera, and withdrew my gloves to fish it out of my oilskins. My fingers were wet and cold, and I fumbled wildly. Leaning to one side for a clearer view, I sighted it nicely just as about six star shells were in the air, and took a long shot. As I released the catch to finish, 'A' and 'B' turrets fired again, and I whipped it up once more in an attempt to catch the tracers before they became too vague to distinguish.

Ramsden recalled being bathed in the light of a German star shell, then soaked by a near miss from a salvo of 11-inch shells:

It sent up a column of water which then collapsed all over the bridge and decks, and had, of course, drowned us as well. Still the slogging match continued, flash for flash, round for round.

The Battle of North Cape

By 18:00 hours the *Scharnhorst* was too far away for the radar operators on board the *Duke of York* to make out the fall of shot on their screens, and for the gunnery lookouts it was impossible to do more than take the bearing of the *Scharnhorst*'s guns when she fired. Fraser requested Commander Meyrick's destroyers to observe the fall of shot for the flagship. After all, at a range of 12,000 yards (6 nautical miles), they could do little else. Even then, by 18:16 hours, Lieutenant Commander Clouston in *Scorpion* was forced to report: 'Can only see occasional splashes due to smoke.' This was naval gunnery practised in the most extreme of conditions.

At 18:20 hours the *Scharnhorst* ceased firing: at 19,000 yards (9½ nautical miles) the range was simply too far for her visual gunnery observers to see anything in the darkness. The 5.25-inch guns on board the *Duke of York* were still firing, although they were at extreme range. All their fire did was give the observers on the *Scharnhorst* a clearer point of aim. However, by 18:20 hours even the firing of these guns (using older non flash-free propellant) was of little help to the German gun directors. The *Scharnhorst* had evidently switched on her radar at some stage early in the battle, and after her turn away to the south-east the stern-mounted FuMo 27 Seetakt radar would have helped ease the problem of gunnery fire control in such poor conditions. But at 19,000 yards it was no longer of much use.

At 18:19 hours, Admiral Bey sent another, rather more optimistic signal to Kiel and Narvik. It read: 'the enemy is firing by radar at a range of more than 18,000 metres. Position AC4965, course 110°, speed 26 knots.' It seemed as if Bey had escaped. After all, although the battlecruiser was damaged, only one of her guns was out of action, her engines were intact, and she was still steaming at full speed. Within minutes she would be clear of the enemy guns. That was when the miracle happened. At 18:20 hours, one of the last salvos fired by the *Duke of York* before the enemy pulled out of range managed to successfully straddle the target. Better still, at least one of her 14-inch shells scored a direct hit on the *Scharnhorst*. Petty Officer Gödde was almost killed:

One shell ripped up the forepart of the ship, and I was thrown on to the deck by the force of the explosion. Kapitän-zur-See Hintze, who emerged from the admiral's bridge to survey the damage,

Day 7: Sunday 26 December 1943

was wounded in the face by splinters, but it did not stop him from coming over to me and helping me to my feet. For a second time he asked if I was hurt, but again I'd been lucky. He then sent me over to the starboard range finder to find out why the men were not answering calls. They were all dead. The rangefinder had been blown to pieces.

In fact the damage was much more extensive than it appeared to Hintze or Gödde. The hit just forward of the bridge appeared to have caused very little significant damage. However, another shell also penetrated the armoured belt of the ship on its starboard side, just astern from the funnel. It exploded in the starboard machinery space, causing damage to the battlecruiser's No. 1 (starboard) boiler room. Although the damage didn't appear significant at first, it severed a crucial steam pipe, and as a result boiler pressure fell away rapidly. On the admiral's bridge, Able Seaman (Matrosenobergefreiter) Hubert Witte, who was serving as a runner, noticed the speed recorder in front of him dropping from 29 knots down to 22 knots. The *Scharnhorst* was in danger of losing her advantage of speed.

At one point an announcement was made, claiming, 'Torpedo hit in Boiler Room Number One – speed 8 knots,' which may not have been accurate, but certainly reflected the gravity of the situation. However, somehow the Chief Engineering Officer, Korvettenkapitän König, managed to stop the loss of more steam pressure, and effected emergency repairs to the boiler by cross-connecting the steam piping. Within minutes he was able to send a message to Hintze on the bridge: 'I can maintain 22 knots, we will make it yet.' A relieved Hintze replied, 'Bravo! Keep it up!' But the *Scharnhorst* had lost her commanding lead, and with her top speed reduced to 22 knots, the British pursuers now had a chance to catch up.

It was some time before this change of fortune was noticed on the British ships. On the *Duke of York* Captain Russell and Admiral Fraser had their own problems, because at 18:24 hours – just four minutes after directing her crucial last salvo – the Type 284 fire control radar, which served her 14-inch guns, broke down, forcing the battleship to cease fire. According to Crawford an air of despondency settled on the battleship's bridge as it 'appeared that, despite undoubted hits, the enemy would escape with her superior speed'. The

The Battle of North Cape

two ships were now 21,400 yards (10½ miles) apart and the chance to inflict a lucky hit on the *Scharnhorst* now appeared to have gone. The destroyers were still 12,000 yards astern of the enemy battlecruiser, and it seemed as if nothing could prevent the *Scharnhorst* from escaping.

At 18:40 hours it seemed as if Admiral Fraser had given up the chase. He signalled Burnett, saying: 'I see little hope of catching *Scharnhorst* and am proceeding to support convoy.' In effect, it was an admission of failure. Then someone noticed that the destroyers seemed to be gaining on the *Scharnhorst*. As Lieutenant Leach in the flagship put it:

> Steadily, gallingly the range counters clicked up as the enemy drew away. I cannot adequately describe the growing frustration of those few who were in a position to realise what was happening; to have achieved surprise, got so close, apparently done so well, and all for nothing as the enemy outpaced us into the night. The resultant despondency was profound. But then suddenly the range steadied, then started to close. Had we done it after all?

It soon became clear that the *Scharnhorst* was gradually losing the race. The despondency on board the *Duke of York* soon changed to elation as Fraser and his staff watched Commander Meyrick's four destroyers edge forward towards the *Scharnhorst*. By that stage *Savage* and *Saumarez* were still about 9,000 yards (4½ nautical miles) astern of the *Scharnhorst* to the north-west, while *Scorpion* and *Stord* were 10,000 yards (5 nautical miles) off her starboard beam, to the west-south-west. Meyrick recalled the moment:

> We had only a little speed in excess of the *Scharnhorst*, and to catch up was going to be quite a business. After a time I had a shout from the officer in the plot, who said he was sure we were getting much nearer.

The crew of the battlecruiser spotted the two destroyers to the north-east and began firing at them, while the other two destroyers

Day 7: Sunday 26 December 1943

approached unseen. Meanwhile, Fraser ordered the *Duke of York* to turn towards the *Scharnhorst*, while the *Jamaica* followed in her wake.

On the *Scharnhorst* most of her crew thought that everything was still going well, as did Grossadmiral Schniewind in Kiel. At 18:30 hours, Bey sent a message to him: 'Steering for Tanafjord, square ASC4994, speed 20 knots.' It was almost as if he refused to realise how serious his situation had become. All this while the British destroyers were drawing ever closer. The official *Interrogation Report*, compiled by British Naval Intelligence after the battle, included the following passage:

> it was about 18:30 when shadows were reported on either beam of the *Scharnhorst*. The Gunnery Officer (Korvettenkapitän Bredenbeuker) is said to have remarked that he couldn't fire on shadows, and that he required targets. However, as more than one survivor plaintively remarked, 'The shadows were tangible enough to pump us full of torpedoes.' At about 8,000 yards the shadows materialised into destroyers. There was such a heavy sea running that it was almost impossible to see them from the upper deck.

The German fire was heavy but inaccurate, which was hardly surprising as the destroyers were almost impossible to see, let alone target. Star shells were fired in an attempt to illuminate the small approaching targets, but many of the crews of the smaller guns were still below decks, and therefore the *Scharnhorst* had no effective means of engaging the destroyers at a time when she desperately needed all the firepower she could bring to bear. For what good it did, *Savage* and *Saumarez* opened fire with their forward 4.7-inch guns at a range of 7,000 yards (3½ nautical miles) – a gesture to improve the morale of their own crews more than a means of hitting the enemy. *Scorpion* and *Stord* held their fire, until they were finally detected at a range of 6,000 yards, and the *Scharnhorst* opened fire with star shell. Commander Owen, Gunnery Officer of the Norwegian destroyer *Stord*, passed on the order to prepare the torpedoes:

> The gunner rushed to ready the torpedo tubes. The range grew shorter with terrifying speed – 3,000, 2,500, 1,900, 1,800 metres.

The Battle of North Cape

I could hardly believe my eyes. There, right in front of me, lay that awesome steel giant.

Star shells dazzled the crews of the four destroyers but they were now fully committed to a torpedo attack.

Then, at around 18:50 hours, the *Scharnhorst* altered course to starboard, presumably in an attempt to present a smaller target to the oncoming destroyers, which were then approaching from '6-o-clock' and '9-o-clock'. In effect, she was trying to thread her way between the two groups, presenting as small a target as possible to them as she did so. This also meant she was now on a south-westerly course (approximately 220°) and making a speed through the water of around 20 knots. *Scorpion* and *Stord* had been heading north-west, but around 18:40 hours they began curving round to the north. This meant that, before her turn, the *Scharnhorst* was virtually sailing on a collision course with them and directly away from the *Savage* and *Saumarez*. As she turned she presented her port beam to the two southern destroyers, which were now almost directly east of her.

At 18:52 hours the *Scorpion* and *Stord* launched a spread of eight 21-inch torpedoes each, from a range of approximately 2,100 yards. That meant the destroyers were within a mile of the looming battle-cruiser when they fired: at that range the torpedoes would take less than 90 seconds to reach their target. On the *Scorpion*'s bridge, Yeoman Mills recalled that the *Scharnhorst* resembled

> some huge black shadow, which threw out spasmodic gun flashes. The ship was dead silent as we closed and as we turned to fire a young ordinary seaman manning the Oerlikon gun under the bridge suddenly yelled out 'Out wires and fenders, port side' – the standard precautionary order when coming alongside another ship!

Of the sixteen torpedoes fired by the two destroyers, probably only one hit the battlecruiser, although some observers claimed three successful hits. As Commander Owen on the *Stord* put it: 'Some thought they heard three, others a succession of underwater explosions.' The whole situation was confusing, as on the far side of the *Scharnhorst* the other two destroyers – *Savage* and *Saumarez* – were launching an

Day 7: Sunday 26 December 1943

almost simultaneous attack. It is more than likely that the expectant destroyer crews claimed virtually all the hits as their own during those tense few minutes. To fire, the destroyers were heading north, or even slightly to the north-north-west, but as soon as their torpedoes were released they veered off to starboard, onto a north-easterly course. That meant they swung their sterns into the oncoming waves, and as the *Stord* made her turn away a huge wave swept one of her crew overboard, and damaged the port depth charge racks.

In these conditions it was hardly a textbook attack. After her turn the battlecruiser was on a virtually reciprocal course for a few seconds, before turning away to present her stern to the attackers. Also, the *Scharnhorst* and the destroyers were passing each other at a combined speed of around 40 knots, which made a hit even harder to achieve. It was hardly surprising that only one confirmed hit was achieved – claimed by the crew of the *Scorpion*. After the battle, Captain Storheill of the *Stord* was unable to claim any definite hits during the torpedo attack. Survivors from the *Scharnhorst* recall that there was only one explosion at that stage, the torpedo striking the ship just forward of the bridge, on her port side.

On the far side of the battlecruiser, *Savage* and *Saumarez* were slowly overhauling the battlecruiser from astern, or rather from a fine angle on her starboard quarter. However, when the *Scharnhorst* made her turn to port they suddenly found themselves on a collision course, with the range dropping dramatically. In order to fire their torpedoes the destroyers needed to present their beam to the target, so at around 18:52 hours they both turned in succession onto a north-easterly course – a reciprocal one to the *Scharnhorst*. On the *Jamaica*, Lieutenant Ramsden watched the attack:

> I confess to having completely forgotten about them (the destroyers) until then, but now I blessed their presence. There was a strange lull in the gunfire. Everyone was on tiptoe, straining to catch the first signs of their attack.

The range was now around 2,500 yards. Before she could fire her torpedoes the *Saumarez* was hit. An 11-inch shell fired from the *Scharnhorst*'s 'Caesar' turret struck the destroyer's tiny director tower, but amazingly it passed through it without exploding. However, the tiny ship was showered with splinters, mauling a crewman of one of her torpedo launchers and piercing her deck, causing havoc in her engine room. Her starboard engine was damaged by debris, reducing her speed to 10 knots at exactly the moment when she needed all her power to escape the German battlecruiser's heavy guns. Eleven men were killed and the same number seriously injured.

Still, the *Saumarez* was committed to the attack, and at 18:53 hours Lieutenant Commander Walmsley gave the order to fire. The two destroyers fired virtually simultaneously. The *Samaurez* only managed to fire a spread of four torpedoes, as the shell-hit meant that one of her two torpedo launchers was damaged and out of action. But *Scorpion* fired a full spread, which meant a dozen lethal 21-inch torpedoes were now powering their way towards the *Scharnhorst*, which was now beam on and presenting a perfect target. At that range it took two long minutes before the torpedoes reached their target, but as soon as they released their salvo the destroyers turned away to the north, putting as much distance between themselves and the battlecruiser as they could. As they did so they opened up on the *Scharnhorst* with their small 4.7-inch guns – they could inflict very little damage, but the firing boosted the morale of the destroyer crews.

Of this spread of three destroyers, at least three torpedoes hit their target, one hitting the *Scharnhorst* on her starboard bow, a second a little astern of the funnel, and the third in the stern. The time was approximately 18:55 hours. Water poured into the steering compartment and other stern spaces, and while the flooding was contained, the torpedo-hit inevitably caused damage to the battlecruiser's propulsion system. Speed dropped again, this time to around 8 to 10 knots. Within a minute the *Scharnhorst* had been hit simultaneously to port and starboard by four torpedoes, with a total explosive charge of 3,240 pounds of Torpex ('Torpex' stood for Torpedo Explosive, a type of explosive that was half as powerful again as conventional high explosives). Few warships could survive such a battering but the *Scharnhorst* seemed to shrug off the damage and continue the fight.

In fact the damage was more severe than it looked to the British. Gunner Helmut Backhaus claimed that:

> there was the sound of approaching torpedoes. Then came the explosions. A tremor ran through the ship, and she gave a great

Day 7: Sunday 26 December 1943

heave. It was like an earthquake.... We no longer stood a chance.

Helmut Feifer was a messenger for the after damage control party, so he was stationed towards the stern of the ship, where one of the torpedoes hit: 'I felt the ship give a violent shudder. The lights went out – it was tar-black.' He had just delivered a message when the torpedoes hit, and he immediately headed back to his station. He recalled:

There had been a bloodbath in my division: all my pals (of the damage control party) were dead – only one was still alive. He was sitting on a crate of potatoes, leaning with his back to the wall, but his clothes were on fire and his hair was a fiery torch. I put out the flames and called for help. Men came running from 'Caesar' turret and together we carried him out. His suffering was beyond description.

As it was impossible to work out how bad the damage was in the stern compartments, the order came to seal the aftermost watertight doors. Some twenty-five engineers were still back there, but they had to be sacrificed to save the rest of the crew. They must have died within minutes as the stern filled with icy water. On the bridge wing, Petty Officer Gödde had his own problems to deal with as the destroyers peppered the superstructure with small calibre shells:

A torpedo struck, bringing the ship to a momentary standstill. Then we were hit by a small calibre shell that blew the range-finder from its mounting. I was standing just behind it, and both leads of my headphones were cut, but I was unhurt.

He was ordered to the bridge, where he saw Konter-Admiral Bey and Kapitän-zur-See Hintze trying to make sense of the mounting chaos.

At that moment the *Duke of York* opened fire again, and scored a direct hit with her first salvo. For the past twenty minutes the *Duke of York*, followed by the *Jamaica*, had sailed directly towards the *Scharnhorst*, closing the range. The Type 284 fire control radar on

The Battle of North Cape

the battleship had been repaired, and now detailed fire control solutions were being passed to the 14-inch guns using both radar and optical sighting reports. As the flagship's gunnery log noted:

> The smoke and the flashes of enemy gunfire afforded fleeting points of aim. The destroyers were now in full cry, and the enemy appeared as a dark source in the centre of a veritable mass of diverging and converging tracer and gunfire.

At 19:00 hours the *Duke of York* swung 90° to starboard, onto a southeasterly course, to clear her 'A arc'. The *Jamaica* followed her, and at 19:01 hours the battleship opened fire. On the *Jamaica*, Lieutenant Ramsden recalled the moment:

> We turned to starboard, the turrets following round so that both ships presented a full broadside. I think I yelled 'Stand by again!' over the headphones, but my words were drowned by the deafening crash of gunfire. The tracer now appeared almost horizontal, as flat was the trajectory as they rushed like fireflies to converge at a point in the darkness. Suddenly – a bright glow, and in it the enemy was to be clearly seen for a brief moment. 'She's hit! My God, we've got her!' I was yelling like one possessed. We were cheering in the director. All over the ship a cheer went up, audible above the gunfire.

The *Duke of York* and the *Jamaica* had opened up at a range of 10,400 yards (just over 5 nautical miles), and their gunnery was deadly accurate. The 14-inch guns of the *Duke of York* scored a direct hit on the *Scharnhorst*'s quarterdeck, causing the explosions seen by Ramsden. Both ships reloaded, then kept on firing. Lieutenant Ramsden reported what he saw to his shipmates below decks: 'I told them as calmly as I could that we could see our shells setting her on fire, and that both the *Duke of York* and ourselves were hitting, and hitting hard.'

Over the next twenty-five minutes the *Duke of York* fired a broadside per minute into the *Scharnhorst*, straddling her with all but four salvos. Each salvo was composed of ten 14-inch shells, and at that range many of these struck the battlecruiser on a virtually horizontal

Day 7: Sunday 26 December 1943

trajectory, pounding her into scrap. It was a demolition job – a steady, relentless display of raw firepower. On the British flagship Wing Commander Compston watched the destruction of the enemy from the plotting table at the back of the admiral's bridge:

> In the short periods between broadsides and the enemy's salvos, there was complete quiet in this little space high up in the super-structure – the cranium as it were of the brain behind the action. So quiet were the discussions that one might have imagined that they were carrying out an ordinary practice shoot at the battle practice target.

Flag Lieutenant Merry watched the same spectacle, standing beside Admiral Fraser:

> Every time we hit her it was just like stoking a huge fire, with flames and sparks flying up the chimney. Every time a salvo landed, there was this great gust of flame, roaring up into the air, just as though we were prodding a huge fire with a poker. Tremendous, unforgettable sight.

The contrast with conditions on the *Scharnhorst* could hardly have been more marked. On the *Scharnhorst* neither the 6-inch nor even the 14-inch shells appear to have penetrated her armoured belt – the range was very short, which meant that, instead of angling down to pierce her less well protected deck, the shells slammed into the foot-thick belt of Krupp steel that protected the sides of her hull. However, other shells struck above the belt, hitting her gun turrets, her super-structure and turning her upper deck spaces into a twisted tangle of searing hot metal. Shells were exploding inside her superstructure, killing, mangling and destroying anything within their blast area. The *Scharnhorst* was fast becoming a blazing wreck. Strangely enough, inside the armoured citadel many of her crew still had little idea how bad things had become. The engines still appeared to be running, the lighting still worked, and for the most part the crew remained confident that their ship was unsinkable.

The Battle of North Cape

Back on the upper deck, the shells were causing incredible damage. The forward port 150mm (6-inch) gun turret was knocked out, the aircraft hangar was hit again, which started a major fire, and several of the smaller gun mounts were ripped apart. Most of the battle-cruiser's port side deck guns were knocked out, their crews strewn around the upper deck. The forecastle was hit repeatedly, ripping away an anchor and its cable. The chief boatswain went forward to inspect the damage, but was swept over the side by a wave. The superstructure was burning in several places, and passageways were blocked or crushed, making movement through the ship almost impossible. Survivors told of bodies or body parts lying everywhere. Medical teams did what they could, but they were unable to cope with the carnage.

However, all through this the *Scharnhorst* kept firing back with the guns that were still operational. As soon as the *Duke of York* opened fire, the German observers could see her and the *Jamaica* ahead of them. While Hintze swung his ship to starboard, away from this new threat, the guns switched targets and returned fire as best as they could. 'Anton' turret had been knocked out earlier, and 'Bruno' turret was firing under local gunnery control. Only 'Caesar' turret was still operating at full effect. At 19:22 hours the ventilation system of 'Bruno' turret was hit and within minutes its interior was filled with acrid, choking, black smoke. Conditions were virtually impossible for the gun crews. 'Caesar' turret was also still operational, and firing under local control, but it was fast running out of ammunition. Petty Officer Gödde remembers hearing the report that 'Caesar' turret had run out of ammunition, and that 'Bruno' had just one three-gun salvo left. Hintze ordered shells to be moved aft from 'Anton' turret to 'Bruno', but events overtook the ship before this difficult job could be carried out.

The *Scharnhorst* carried two torpedo tubes amidships, one on each side of her hull. The Torpedo Officer, Oberleutnant-zur-See Bosse was seen working his way through the debris to the port side torpedo tube. The *Duke of York* could be seen about 3 nautical miles away, on the battlecruiser's port quarter. He tried to fire a salvo, but only one of the three torpedoes left the damaged launcher – two stuck in their tubes. Given the conditions it was more of a defiant gesture than a serious attempt to engage the British battleship, and the torpedo passed

Day 7: Sunday 26 December 1943

wide of its target. Gunner Günther Sträter, in the remaining 150mm turret on the port side, heard the message from Hintze, relayed from the bridge: 'the heavy guns have been knocked out. Now it's up to you!' With their fire control systems destroyed there was little the *Scharnhorst*'s remaining operational gun crew could do but point their barrels in the general direction of the enemy, fire, and hope for the best.

At about 19:20 Hintze sent one last signal to Kiel: 'We shall fight to the last shell. Long live Germany. Long live the Führer.' The message was repeated to the crew via the ship's intercom – this was the first indication for some of her crew sheltering below decks that the battlecruiser was in serious trouble. Worse was to follow. Five or ten minutes later Hintze made the announcement: 'Take Action Number Five.' That was an emergency measure, which had rarely been practised on board the *Scharnhorst*. It called for all watertight doors to be closed, to reduce the risk of damage from enemy torpedoes and to stop – or at least to slow down – the spread of flooding throughout the ship. In the worst of situations, it slowed the rate at which the ship sank, and therefore bought a little extra time for her crew to abandon ship. In all likelihood Hintze was simply giving a sensible order in the circumstances, as the battlecruiser had already been hit by four torpedoes. His ship was now limping along at 8 or 10 knots, and listing slightly to starboard. The *Scharnhorst* had also altered course to starboard after the torpedoes struck her, and she was now on an east-south-easterly course – steering approximately 115°. Hintze must have realised his ship was now little more than a floating target. Watching from the bridge he must have seen the British cruisers close in to launch a torpedo attack of their own.

Admiral Fraser soon realised that he wasn't going to sink the *Scharnhorst* through gunfire alone. Despite the pounding the battle-cruiser had taken, and the fires raging on her superstructure and upper decks, she was riding no lower in the water. He knew that, as the range was now down to about 3,000 yards (1½ nautical miles), the shell trajectory was virtually horizontal, which meant there was little chance of breaching the *Scharnhorst*'s armoured belt and scoring a penetrating hit against her engines or magazine. She could no longer fight back, but she could float, and she could just about move. The only way to sink her was to use torpedoes.

The Battle of North Cape

At 19:19 hours Fraser ordered the *Jamaica* to: 'Finish her off with torpedoes.' A minute later he sent the same signal to the *Belfast*, which had been steadily approaching the battlecruiser from the north-north-west, and was now 3 miles away. The rest of Rear Admiral Burnett's Force 1 was too far away to take any further part in the action. The *Jamaica* steamed onto a course parallel to the *Scharnhorst*, about 3,000 yards on her starboard beam – well within torpedo range. As the British cruiser made her approach the *Scharnhorst* slowly turned to port, in an attempt to present her stern to the enemy torpedoes. Throughout the manoeuvre the *Jamaica* continued to fire her 6-inch guns at the enemy battlecruiser. As Lieutenant Ramsden put it:

> One 6-inch broadside and then another was fired – straight into her. We couldn't miss at that range – 3,000 yards. I could smell the sweetish smell of burning. It must be the *Scharnhorst*.

At 19:25 hours *Jamaica* fired a spread of three torpedoes from her port launchers as star shells lit up both the British cruiser and her German prey. One torpedo misfired and the remaining two missed the target, probably because the *Scharnhorst* had begun her turn to starboard just as they were being fired. Captain Hughes-Hallett then turned his cruiser hard about, to allow his starboard torpedo tubes to bear. Two minutes after the *Jamaica* fired, the *Belfast* launched her own spread of three torpedoes from her starboard launcher. At 19:27 hours she was 5,000 yards (2½ nautical miles) due north of the enemy. This meant that, as the *Scharnhorst* turned, she effectively 'combed' the spread of torpedoes from both cruisers. Of the five torpedoes fired, none hit their target.

Meanwhile, reinforcements had arrived. Commander Fisher's 6th Destroyer Division, which had been attached to Force 1 early that morning, had accompanied Burnett's cruisers as they chased the *Scharnhorst* southwards. They were some 8 nautical miles north of the *Scharnhorst* when she was hit by the lucky salvo from the *Duke of York* at 18:20 hours, steering a south-easterly course, which was roughly parallel to the German battlecruiser. For the past hour they had fought their way through the oncoming gale as they worked their way closer, and by the time Fraser ordered his cruisers to fire

Day 7: Sunday 26 December 1943

torpedoes at the *Scharnhorst* they were in a position to launch their own attack. The four destroyers split into two sub-divisions, Fisher in *Musketeer* leading the *Matchless*, while Commander Lee-Barber, in *Opportune*, was followed by *Virago*.

At 19:30 hours Admiral Fraser gave Fisher the order he'd been waiting for, and the two pairs of destroyers surged forward to launch their attack. The plan was for Fisher's sub-division to attack the battlecruiser from her port side, while Lee-Barber launched his attack from off her starboard beam. By the time they were in position the *Scharnhorst* had completed a lazy turn to port, and she was now steering a south-westerly course – roughly on a bearing of 245°. That made it relatively easy for *Musketeer* and *Matchless* to slip past her and take station on her port quarter. *Opportune* and *Virago* had the easier approach, and took station to the north of the battlecruiser, about 2,100 yards (a little over 1 nautical mile) off her starboard quarter. *Opportune* was the first to launch her torpedoes, at 19:31 hours. She fired a spread of four, and about 90 seconds later her crew were rewarded with a single hit. She launched another spread of four torpedoes two minutes later, and may have hit the battlecruiser again.

On the far side of the *Scharnhorst*, *Musketeer* fired a spread of four torpedoes at 19:33 hours, from just 1,000 yards. Fisher turned away towards the south, but recalled seeing 'the columns of white spray go up alongside the target, as some of them hit.' The destroyer later claimed two torpedo hits, between the funnel and the mainmast on the *Scharnhorst*'s port side. *Matchless* had problems with the torpedo launcher, and she was forced to turn away with her torpedoes still in their tubes. But a minute after *Musketeer* fired, *Virago* launched her full spread of torpedoes – or at least seven of them, as one failed to launch. Her inexperienced crew still managed to score two more hits. That means in just three minutes the *Scharnhorst* had been hit by another five torpedoes – two on her port side, and three to starboard.

The survivors of the *Scharnhorst* all had hazy recollections of those moments when their ship received its death blows. One torpedo jammed 'Bruno' turret, which stopped any attempt to replenish her stocks of shells from the magazine of 'Anton' turret. The blast jammed the turret hatches, so of all the men serving the guns and magazine of 'Bruno' turret, only one man – Ordinary Seaman (Matrosengefreiter) Rudi Birke – survived: the rest went down with the ship. Another

The Battle of North Cape

torpedo hit the *Scharnhorst* amidships, and the damage control party sent to inspect the flooding found their way blocked by wreckage. The water continued to pour into the ship, limited only by the watertight doors that had not been wrenched off by the torpedo explosions. Fires now raged through the engine rooms, and the ship began to list to starboard even more heavily than before.

Finally, it was the turn of the *Jamaica* again. By 19:37 she had turned around, and now lay 3,700 yards (just less than 2 nautical miles) off the port beam of the battlecruiser. Captain Hughes-Hallet noticed that, in the twelve minutes since his cruiser had launched her last torpedo attack, the small-calibre fire from the battlecruiser had slackened appreciably. Of course it didn't help that the *Scharnhorst* was now heeling over and most of her guns were incapable of bearing on the *Jamaica*. The cruiser fired three torpedoes, an event recalled by Petty Officer Mahoney, manning the starboard tubes:

> Our tubes were fired one after the other. My work was done, so I ordered the tubes trained fore and aft, and then waited for the explosions – if we hit. Then one explosion, and then another.

These last torpedoes must have struck the exposed lower hull of the battlecruiser's port side at around 19:40 hours. Everyone on the deck of the *Jamaica* peered into the cloud of smoke, hoping to see what effect their last spread might have had. The *Jamaica*'s Torpedo Officer, Lieutenant Commander Chavasee recalled the moment:

> We then did another swing, and fired three more from our starboard tubes. The enemy seemed to resent this, and blazed away with his secondary armament and close-range weapons, but most of his stuff went over our heads. When the smoke cleared we saw the *Scharnhorst* lying on its side. She looked like a whale that had just come up for air, except that she was ablaze from stem to stern.

It seems likely that the two torpedoes ripped into the after port side of the *Scharnhorst*. If the destroyers hadn't finished her, then the *Jamaica* had.

Day 7: Sunday 26 December 1943

At about 19:40 hours Kapitän-zur-See Hintze gave the order to 'Abandon Ship', although some survivors claim the order came through a little earlier. Petty Officer Gödde recalls:

> Several more torpedo hits, nearly all on the starboard side. We were heeling over more and more. Last ship's operational order was in plain language – 'Captain's Order – Abandon Ship! All hands topside! Put on life jackets! Prepare to jump overboard!'

According to Gödde, Hintze ushered the twenty-five or so survivors on the bridge outside, ordering them to save their own lives. Gödde also saw the captain give his own life jacket to a sailor who had lost his, claiming that he was an excellent swimmer. Gödde continues:

> Still more torpedoes tore into the ship, giving her a more severe list. On the deck, order and discipline reigned – you could scarcely hear a single loud word.

Gödde also saw the Executive Officer, Commander Dominik, 'a tall figure on the upper deck',

> calmly helping the hundreds of seamen who had reached the deck to climb over the railing. Above, the Captain checked our life jackets once again, and then the Captain and Admiral clasped hands in a final farewell.

It was clear that the *Scharnhorst* was finished. After the final torpedo hits from the *Jamaica*, the *Scharnhorst* heeled over rapidly, and her bows were now completely submerged. In his after 105mm (4.1-inch) turret, Ordinary Seaman (Matrosengefreiter) Sträter heard the order to abandon ship and filed out on deck with the rest of the gun crew. Chief Gunner Wibbelhoff and Senior Gunner's Mate Moritz stayed behind, choosing to remain at their posts until the end. The last Sträter saw of them, Wibbelhoff was resuming his position on the gunlayer's seat and lighting a cigarette. They were still there when the ship sank.

Crewmen abandoned ship to both port and starboard, but as the ship was capsizing the jump from the exposed port hull of the ship

The Battle of North Cape

was almost suicidal. For that matter, so was the jump into the water from starboard – several survivors told how sailors threw themselves from the superstructure only to hit the deck below. Ordinary Seaman (Matrosengefreiter) Helmut Boekhoff heard the order to abandon ship:

> I went up to the tower, to the crow's nest, to get out, and by the time I got there the ship was already lying on her starboard side, so we had a hard job to get out [...] I could see shipmates jumping from the searchlight tower right down into the ship. When they hit the water they were killed instantly, because of the steel just beneath the surface. I went over to the starboard side, and when I got there she just flopped over, and I was thrown into the water. The first thing I thought about was a raft, as I had no lifejacket – I didn't have time to get one. I saw things floating about, and I then saw a piece of wood, which I grabbed – it was one of the gunnery floats from the pom-poms.

At approximately 19:45 hours the *Scharnhorst* finally heeled over completely onto her starboard side, and slipped beneath the waves, bow first. Gunner Sträter was in the water:

> The ship heeled over onto her side and sank by the bow. The propellers were still turning as they came out of the water. Indeed, they were all turning rather fast – there was way on the ship right until the end (i.e. her engines were still driving her forward). In the water the crew were trying to find rafts. Those who found places in them sang both stanzas of the song 'No roses bloom on a sailor's grave.' I heard no cries for help from the water – everything happened smoothly, without the slightest panic.

Petty Officer Gödde supported this view of the crew's spirit. He made it into the water, but he and a colleague were sucked under when the ship sank. He made it back to the surface, but never saw his companion again. The seas were rough, and he slipped off a wooden grating he came across, but finally found a raft to clamber into. The raft was filled with men cheering: 'Three cheers for the *Scharnhorst*!' He heard sailors say they had seen the captain, swimming without a

Day 7: Sunday 26 December 1943

lifejacket, but by that time snow had started to fall heavily, making visibility difficult. At least the oil from the hull helped flatten the surface of the water, making conditions almost bearable in the small raft. Gunner Boekhoff recalled the scene:

> As she went down I felt this great tremor in my stomach and legs. There was a big explosion below water. At the time all I thought about was getting away. When I looked around I saw these shipmates – they're swimming between all these bits of debris, still shouting 'Heil Hitler' and '*Scharnhorst* hurrah' over and over again. I thought: 'What a waste.'

A mile or so away to the north and south, all the British ships saw was a cloud of smoke, which obscured everything inside it. Many had heard a series of dull underwater explosions at 19:45 hours – almost certainly the sound made by the battlecruiser as she rolled over and sank. On the *Duke of York* the radar operators actually saw the *Scharnhorst* go under. Lieutenant Cox recalled that at around 19:45 hours:

> You could see the echo that had been the *Scharnhorst* gradually getting smaller and smaller – a little golden streak [...] and as we watched it going smaller it eventually just disappeared, and we knew the *Scharnhorst* had sunk.

On the bridge Admiral Fraser was still sceptical, and twelve minutes later, at 19:57 hours, he ordered: 'Clear area of target except for ship with torpedoes and destroyer with searchlight.' He was still taking no chances. On the *Belfast*, Rear Admiral Burnett radioed Lieutenant Commander Clouston in *Scorpion*, asking him if the *Scharnhorst* was still afloat. Nobody knew what was going on inside the pall of smoke.

At 19:48 hours *Belfast* edged closer to the smoke, her crew hoping to launch a second torpedo attack. They fired another star shell to illuminate the target, but the men could see nothing through the smoke and snow. At 19:51 *Scorpion*'s Lieutenant Commander Clouston signalled: 'A lot of wreckage on sea. Am closing now.' Then, just after 20:00 hours, lookouts on the *Belfast* spotted the thick oil slick as the smoke began to dissipate, accompanied by the strong smell of burnt

The Battle of North Cape

oil. Then they saw the rafts. As Captain Parham recalled: 'We came across a raft of shouting, if not screaming, German sailors. Rather a horrid sight, really.' The sea was covered with bodies, some alive, but most dead. Screams and cries could be heard in the darkness. It was now clear the *Scharnhorst* had sunk. On the *Scorpion*, Able Seaman Baxendale helped drape a scrambling net over the side:

> We were the only ship there with a searchlight, so we swung round and came back ... we switched the searchlight on and there they were, floating all around, everywhere [...] It was terrible, they were all like bloody seagulls, bobbing up and down in the water on rafts.

Gunner Backhaus was on one of these rafts, and he saw the searchlight:

> They saw us and drew nearer. We were frozen to the bone, and many of us were unable to keep a grip on the ropes they threw down to us. I tied the end of a rope around my waist and was hauled up. Two men clung on to my legs, wanting to be hauled up with me, but they were unable to hold on. Both fell back into the sea and disappeared.

Most of the survivors told a similar story. On board the *Duke of York* Admiral Fraser was slowly coming to terms with the fact that his enemy had sunk. At 20:04 hours *Scorpion* radioed the flagship to report: 'Am picking up survivors.' Fourteen minutes later Fraser contacted Clouston, asking him: 'Has *Scharnhorst* sunk?' Finally, at 20:30 hours, the signal came back: 'Survivors state that *Scharnhorst* has sunk.' A similar message came from Burnett on the *Belfast*: 'Satisfied that *Scharnhorst* has sunk.' Fraser finally realised that it was all over. He had sunk his opponent. Consequently, at 20:35 hours, Admiral Fraser sent the signal to Scapa Flow, to be forwarded to the Admiralty. In typically understated naval fashion it simply said: '*Scharnhorst* sunk.' In equally understated fashion the acknowledgement came back from the Admiralty an hour later. It read: 'Grand. Well Done.' The great naval struggle was finally over. All that remained was the grim job of picking up survivors.

Aftermath

—◦◦⟨◦⟩◦◦—

When she sailed from the Altenfjord the *Scharnhorst* carried a complement of approximately 1,972 men, including the fifty or so staff of Konter-Admiral Bey, who were embarked at the last minute. One Soviet source places the number as high as 2,029 men. Of these, there were only thirty-six survivors. Nobody knows for certain how many German sailors managed to escape from the sinking ship, but eye witnesses have estimated the numbers to be in the high hundreds.

The Survivors

There may have been as many as 1,000 crewmen who threw themselves clear of the ship. Of these, many would have been sucked under when the *Scharnhorst* sank. Of the rest, the chances of survival would have been slim. Cold water removes heat from the body twenty-five times faster than cold air of the same temperature. Physical activity such as swimming away from a sinking ship or towards a raft greatly increases the rate of heat loss. Statistics show that in those temperatures, a swimmer would lapse into unconsciousness through hypothermia within twenty minutes, and survival time is estimated at around forty minutes, depending on various factors, such as age, physical condition, whether the swimmer was wearing a life jacket or warm clothing, or had managed to find wreckage to cling to. These figures are for so-called 'ideal conditions' – the well-monitored water of a diving tank or swimming pool. But the *Scharnhorst's* sailors were pitched into a freezing, oil-covered sea at night, in the midst of a gale. Many would have been injured and many would have been in a state of shock. Exposure to freezing water could also lead to increased heart rate and blood pressure, which could easily result in cardiac arrest. Even those who reached the relative safety of a raft would have slipped into unconsciousness fairly rapidly. After all, 50 per cent of body heat is lost through the head. These men were lying in pitching rafts, which were half-filled with sloshing, freezing water, and it was snowing heavily.

The British did what they could. The destroyer *Scorpion* picked up thirty survivors, although her commander, Lieutenant Commander Clouston, said that there must have been over 100 men struggling in the water beside the landing nets. Six more were rescued by the destroyer *Musketeer*. Many of these German sailors were too weak to pull themselves out of the water or even grab the lines thrown down from the deck above. The *Scharnhorst*'s Executive Officer, Fregatten-kapitän Dominik, was one of these unfortunate swimmers – he actually had his hands on a lifeline but slipped away from the *Scorpion* into the darkness before he could be rescued. It didn't help that the rough seas were either sweeping people or wreckage against the destroyer, or else away from it, consigning swimmers to a cold, dark death. Conditions would have been much worse if the oil slick hadn't flattened the water a little. The *Scorpion*'s searchlight continued to sweep over the sea, its beam illuminating hundreds of floating bodies.

Petty Officer Gödde watched from the oily water as *Scorpion* stopped upwind of his raft, and allowed herself to drift down towards it. By that time he had been in the water or the raft for about an hour, and he felt himself failing fast. The destroyer crew realised that few of the survivors could climb up the landing net unaided, so they lowered ropes over the side. Gödde was too weak to grasp it, and too frozen to work the bowline loop at the end of it around his waist. He tried and failed four times and was at the point of giving up when another rope was dropped, hitting him in the face. Out of sheer desperation he grasped it with his teeth, and was hauled up the 12 feet between water-line and deck, helped in part by the waves. Eager hands reached down and grabbed him, and he was hauled to safety. He was one of the very few lucky ones.

Once on board, the survivors were tended by their former pro-tagonists. Able Seaman Horton, on board *Matchless*, remembered the scene:

There were six ratings picked up, in a dirty condition, wet through, also covered in oil. Their behaviour was reasonable as

Aftermath

they were glad to be saved and glad to get on board. They were treated like any other survivors that were picked up, taken to a messdeck, given rum to fetch up any oil they may have swallowed, given dry clothing, and put into hammocks in the forward mess.

While the rum might have done little to help men suffering from hypothermia, the other universal British panacea in these situations – hot sweet tea – was literally a life saver.

By 20:40 hours it was clear that the British destroyers could do little more. It had been almost an hour since the *Scharnhorst* had sunk, and the chances of anyone still surviving in the water were now virtually non-existent. The cries for help in the darkness had died away, and all that remained was the debris, the oil, and the lingering smell of burning. Admiral Fraser's big worry was an attack by German U-boats. A British battleship and four cruisers were loitering in the battle area, standing by while the destroyers carried out their rescue mission. He knew that, before she sank, the *Scharnhorst* had sent several radio messages, and he had to assume these included her position. It stood to reason that the German U-boats that had been shadowing Convoy JW 55B would be heading towards the area. He was right: Gruppe Eisenbart was already on its way. Consequently, at 20:40 hours, Admiral Fraser gave the order to call off the search for survivors.

On board the *Sheffield*, Lieutenant Walker summed up the mood:

One couldn't help but feel sorry for those who had perished. It was a cold, dark night, with little chance of survival in those icy waters. However, it might just as easily have been one, or indeed all of us.

When the news reached the escorts of Convoy JW 55B there was rejoicing, but the mood soon changed. Sub Lieutenant Carey, on the *Onslaught*, recalled:

After a brief cheer at the final sinking, our sailors fell silent, reflecting with real pity on the fate of so many of that green ship's company, consigned, in the Arctic twilight, and with little hope of rescue, to the wintry and unwelcome sea. There was almost tangible compassion …

After a brief radio exchange with Rear Admiral Burnett, Admiral Fraser ordered the entire fleet to set a course for the Kola Inlet, although Burnett was first ordered to make contact with Convoy JW 55B. The convoy was considered reasonably safe from attack, but Force 1 (now reinforced by the *Jamaica*) and Force 2 would be able to reinforce it, if it were attacked by U-boats. The *Duke of York* would steer east-north-east, and would rendezvous with Force 1 off the entrance to the inlet. The majority of the British ships headed away from the battle area at 20 knots. But the damaged *Saumarez* could only manage 8 knots, although she was later able to increase her speed. She was joined by *Savage* and *Scorpion*, who provided her with an anti-submarine escort as she limped eastwards towards the Russian anchorage. At noon the following day Lieutenant Commander Walmsley and the crew of the *Saumarez* buried their dead at sea, and by 22:30 hours on 27 December the battered destroyer was safely tied up alongside the jetty at Vaenga, on the eastern side of the Kola Inlet. There her injured were tended, and her damage repaired.

Convoy JW 55B entered Kola Inlet at 10:30 hours on the morning of 29 December. The last leg of the voyage was not without incident. The convoy had been shadowed by German aircraft on 27 and 28 December, but there was no sign of any U-boat activity. That was only because Gruppe Eisenbart had been ordered south in a futile attempt to lend support to the *Scharnhorst*, and was therefore unable to regain contact with the convoy. Meanwhile, two ships had managed to drop out of the convoy during the night of 26–27 December. While the *Ocean Valour* was located and shepherded back into formation, the troublesome *Ocean Gypsy* never rejoined the convoy, and finally made it safely into Kola Inlet some ten hours behind her fellow merchantmen.

With the exception of Commander Meyrick and his trio of destroyers, the rest of Admiral Fraser and Rear Admiral Burnett's forces arrived in the Kola Inlet a little after dawn on 27 December. The Soviet Port Commander, Admiral Golovko expressed his delight at the victory, but complained about the need to provide Fraser's ships with 10,000 tons of fuel. He also questioned the way the British refused

Aftermath

to hand over their prisoners. On the morning after the battle, the survivors on board *Scorpion* had been questioned by the destroyer's first officer, and the valuables taken off them when they were rescued were returned. A more extensive interview would have to wait until the prisoners were transferred to the *Duke of York*, but the British were keen to discover the German version of the battle.

By mid-afternoon the *Scorpion* was anchored in the Kola Inlet, and the survivors were brought on deck. Each was issued with a duffel coat, which suggested to them that they were about to be put ashore, and handed over to the Soviets. When a Soviet tug came alongside with marines on board the small party grew even more restless, and they refused to cooperate. A German-speaking officer was found, who assured the prisoners that they were simply being transferred to the flagship, and would be taken back to Britain in her. The relief was palpable, and one English-speaking survivor – Gunner Johann Merkle – thanked the British officer on behalf of his comrades. The survivors gave three cheers to their rescuers before clambering on board the Soviet tug. Within an hour they were safely ensconced on board the *Duke of York*, where the four wounded survivors were taken to the sick bay, and the rest led to their temporary quarters, a forward messdeck. To the British, these men were not so much prisoners as survivors, and were treated accordingly.

That evening Admiral Fraser invited Rear Admiral Burnett and all his captains to a celebration dinner, where the officers exchanged accounts of the battle, and marvelled at their lack of casualties. During this last engagement some 2,195 shells of various calibres had been fired at the enemy battlecruiser, including no fewer than eighty broadsides from the *Duke of York*'s 14-inch guns. The total number of British casualties amounted to twenty-six men killed and as many wounded, two of which subsequently died of their injuries. Of these almost half the casualties were from the *Saumarez*. Another casualty was Olga, the reindeer presented to Rear Admiral Burnett just a few days before. The gunfire drove her into a maddened frenzy inside the *Belfast*'s hangar, and she had to be put down. That night Admiral Golovko's staff arrived on board the flagship to present Admiral Fraser with a slightly more practical present – a fur hat and coat. However, despite the removal of such a serious threat to the Murmansk convoys the Russians generally remained as suspicious and uncooperative as ever.

The Battle of North Cape

At 18:00 hours on 28 December the *Duke of York* and the *Jamaica* sailed for Scapa Flow, accompanied by seven destroyers. Burnett led the rest of the force home the following day, although *Saumarez* remained at Vaenga for another week. The navigational log of the battleship shows there was no truth in the claim by Petty Officer Gödde that the British flagship stopped to lay a wreath in the waters where the *Scharnhorst* sank. Like several of his claims, they were designed to please his German superiors rather than reflect exactly what happened. The return voyage was wholly uneventful, and on New Year's Day 1944 Admiral Fraser's force arrived at the Home Fleet's wartime anchorage of Scapa Flow. Lieutenant Ramsden of the *Jamaica* recalled the voyage home:

> The southward trip to Scapa was eventful only in the weather. A typical gale force wind from the north-west set up heavy seas, and most of our seaboats on the boat deck were severely damaged. It was an uncomfortable journey, and bitterly cold.

The welcome in Scapa Flow more than made up for the discomfort of the voyage home. According to Ramsden:

> We made Hoxa Gate and steamed slowly into the Flow, battle ensigns flying, the *Duke of York* ahead and our destroyers astern ... It was an impressive and unforgettable experience, passing through the Fleet to our anchorage, each ship's company massed on deck, cheering as we came abreast of them.

Journalist Arthur Oakeshott offered an even more colourful description:

> Suddenly out of the murk to the norrard appeared the *Duke of York* with smoke-blackened 14-inch guns, flying her shell-torn battle ensign, and cramming almost every piece of bunting in the ship.

A flood of congratulatory telegrams were waiting for Fraser, including messages from the King, from Churchill, Roosevelt, Stalin and just about every Allied admiral there was. Further accolades would follow. Admiral Fraser was awarded the Order of the Bath (GCB), Burnett

Aftermath

was given a knighthood (KCB), and a smattering of Distinguished Service Orders (DSOs) and Distinguished Service Medals (DSMs) were awarded to the most deserving participants in the battle below flag rank.

In Kiel, Generaladmiral Schniewind feared the worst, and by the evening of 26 December he realised that the *Scharnhorst* had been sunk. In fact, two signals were transmitted that evening, an expression of thanks from Adolf Hitler, and another from Grossadmiral Dönitz, which said that: 'Your heroic battle for Germany's victory and greatness will be an example for all time.' By the time these signals were sent the *Scharnhorst* lay at the bottom of the Barents Sea. On the morning of 27 December the U-boats of Gruppe Eisenbart reached the last known location of the *Scharnhorst*, but all that was left was a patch of oil on the water. The chances of finding any survivors were non-existent, so any further search was abandoned.

On 29 December the news of the sinking was broadcast over German radio. A shocked nation mourned the loss, but the radio spokesman, Admiral Lützow, summed up the national mood:

We pay homage to our comrades who died a seaman's death, in a heroic battle against a superior enemy. The *Scharnhorst* now rests on the field of honour.

They were fine words, especially if you didn't imagine just how cold and lonely a seaman's death might be. The final act of the *Scharnhorst* drama was played out in Germany, where Schniewind and Dönitz did whatever was necessary to evade responsibility for the debacle. As Konter-Admiral Bey went down with his ship, then he made a suitable scapegoat. The Kriegsmarine commander told Hitler that if Bey had shown a little more aggression, then the mission would have succeeded, and the *Scharnhorst* would have survived. These two naval leaders behaved with far less dignity than the thirty-six survivors of the *Scharnhorst*. With the exception of one sailor, who was repatriated by the Red Cross, the rest spent the remainder of the conflict as prisoners-of-war in Canada and the United States. The majority were sent to Louisiana, where they aided the American economy by picking cotton. They were repatriated after the war and returned home to a very different Germany than the one they had left.

List of German Survivors

There were thirty-six survivors from the *Scharnhorst*, the average age being twenty-one years.

Name	Rank	Duty Station	Age
Johann Achilles	Stoker, 1st Class *(Maschinenobergefreiter)*	Turbine Room	23
Willi Alsen	Able Seaman *(Matrosenobergefreiter)*	Ammunition Supply, Amidships	20
Helmut Backhaus	Able Seaman *(Matrosenobergefreiter)*	105mm gun, Port, Forward	19
Rudi Birke	Ordinary Seaman *(Matrosengefreiter)*	'Bruno' Turret	21
Helmut Boekhoff	Ordinary Seaman	37mm Flak, Starboard	19
Günther Bohle	Able Seaman	105mm gun, Port, Amidships	21
Helmut Feifer	Stoker, 1st Class	Damage Control Party, Amidships	20
Wilhelm Gödde	Petty Officer *(Oberbootsmannsmaat)*	Port Bridge Lookout	33
Heinz Groenewond	Able Seaman	105mm gun, Forward	21
Fritz Hager	Ordinary Seaman	150mm turret, Starboard, Forward	19
Wilhelm Hovedesbrunken	Leading Seaman *(Matrosenhaupgefreiter)*	105mm gun, Starboard, Forward	25
Johann Kastenholz	Acting Petty Officer *(Oberbootsmannsmaat)*	150mm turret, Port, Amidships	26

Name	Rank	Duty Station	Age
Wilhelm Koster	Ordinary Seaman	105mm gun, Starboard, Forward	22
Wilhelm Kruse	Navigator's Yeoman	Admiral's Staff, Bridge	20
Franz Laisz	Stoker, 1st Class	Engine Room	21
Gerhard Lobin	Ordinary Seaman, 2nd Class (*Matrosen*)	Lookout, Forward Director Tower	21
Heinrich Loffenlhoz	Junior Petty Officer (*Bootsmannsmaat*)	150mm turret, Port, Aft	21
Günther Lorke	Ordinary Seaman, 2nd Class (*Matrosen*)	105mm gun, Aft	24
Franz Marko	Stoker, 1st Class	Boiler Room	20
Johann Merkle	Artificer (*Mechanikergefreiter*)	105 mm gun, Port, Amidships	20
Heinz Pfeil	Able Seaman	'Caesar' Turret	24
Max Rauschert	Leading Stoker (*Maschinenhaupgefreiter*)	Engineering Stores, Amidships	24
Ernst Reimann	Artificer	'Caesar' Turret	19
Max Schafer	Ordinary Seaman	105mm gun, Starboard, Amidships	19
Paul Schaffrati	Stoker, 1st Class	Damage Control Party, Amidships	23
Fritz Scherer	Junior Petty Officer	105mm Gun Director, Aft	22
Hermann Schultz	Able Seaman	105mm gun, Starboard, Amidships	19
Heinz Steiniganz	Leading Stoker	Not recorded	22

Name	Rank	Duty Station	Age
Günther Sträter	Ordinary Seaman	105mm gun, Aft	19
Hans Trzembiatowski	Able Seaman	Not recorded	20
Martin Wallek	Able Seaman Shipwright (*Zimmermannsobergefreiter*)	Damage Control Party, Amidships	22
Nicolaus Wiebusch	Able Seaman	37mm Flak, Starboard, Aft	21
Johann Wiest	Artificer	37mm Flak, Port, Amidships	19
Hubert Witte	Able Seaman	Messenger, Bridge	21
Horst Zaubitzer	Artificer	'Caesar' Turret	19
Rolf Zanger	Leading Stoker	Boiler room	24

Aftermath

Conclusion

The sinking of the *Scharnhorst* at the Battle of North Cape was an important victory for British seapower. It could easily be claimed that victory was won by the code-breakers of Bletchley Park. That was the country mansion north of London where coded signals sent using German Enigma encryption machines were decrypted using secret code-breaking machines, devised and supported by expert cryptologists and mathematicians. Codenamed 'Ultra', this enterprise was the greatest intelligence operation of the war. It allowed German signals to be intercepted, decoded, and then passed to senior Allied commanders. Of course, the danger was that it was successful only as long as the Germans didn't realise their 'unbreakable' encryption system had been decoded. Consequently, the dissemination of 'Ultra' information was a risky business.

Both Admiral Fraser and Rear Admiral Burnett were privy to relevant 'Ultra' intelligence, which was passed to them by the Admiralty in London's Whitehall. This meant they knew that the *Scharnhorst* had sailed within hours of its departure, and were able to plot the location of the battlecruiser, its escorting destroyers and the U-boats of Gruppe Eisenbart with some degree of accuracy. It was enough to allow the two Royal Naval commanders to predict Konter-Admiral Bey's next move, and deploy their forces accordingly. By the same token, it presented Fraser with the opportunity to dangle Convoy JW 55B as the bait that would lure the *Scharnhorst* out to sea, while allowing him to keep it reasonably safe – just out of reach of the German Battlegroup.

Once Rear Admiral Burnett's Force 1 was deployed in the path of the *Scharnhorst* in the early morning of 26 December, then the other British advantage made itself felt. While several countries experimented with radar before the war, it was the British who first turned it into a workable reality. Arguably, radar played a crucial part in winning the Battle of Britain, fought in the skies over southern England in the summer of 1940. By that time radar units were being fitted to Royal Naval warships, and as the technology improved, then new radar sets were issued. While the Germans had developed their own radar systems, these were far less sophisticated than those developed by the British. This meant when Force 1 met the *Scharnhorst* that morning, radar would play a crucial part in the ensuing battle.

The Battle of North Cape

By December 1943 the *Scharnhorst* had been fitted with a radar that could detect enemy ships up to 12 miles away – on a good day. It also provided an elementary form of radar fire control for the battlecruiser's main 11-inch guns. By contrast, the British search radar sets had a range almost double that of the *Scharnhorst*, and dedicated fire control radars provided targeting information for gunnery direction. While the Germans enjoyed a superior system of optical range finding and gunnery control, the British enjoyed a significant advantage in radar-guided gunnery, which could be used in addition to, or instead of, gunnery direction using visual means. The British were also lucky. During her first skirmish with the cruisers of Force 1 the *Scharnhorst* lost the use of her forward radar, which greatly reduced the effectiveness of her gunnery. For the most part she was forced to rely on visual gunnery direction – a distinct disadvantage in the snowswept darkness of the Barents Sea.

In the battle that followed, both sides could be criticised for minor errors in deployment or decision-making. After the battle, Grossadmiral Dönitz criticised Konter-Admiral Bey for not being aggressive enough, and for turning away from the British cruisers during the first two skirmishes of the battle. Bey also lost contact with his destroyers, which would have been of inestimable value in the battle. For his part, Rear Admiral Burnett was criticised for errors in deployment, and for losing contact with the *Scharnhorst* after the first skirmish. But Burnett more than made up for any lapses by blocking the *Scharnhorst*'s second attempt to intercept the convoy, and in shadowing the battlecruiser during its long run south. Even Admiral Fraser could be faulted, for not using his advantages of 'Ultra' and radar to better advantage during the opening phase of the final battle. After all, the *Scharnhorst* almost escaped the trap Fraser had set – only a lucky hit by a shell from the *Duke of York* prevented the enemy from getting away.

During that final battle the sinking of the *Scharnhorst* was the result of team effort. Shadowing by the cruisers of Force 1 allowed Force 2 to intercept the enemy warship, although these cruisers were unable to contribute significantly to the battle that followed. The guns of the *Duke of York* then played the major part in preventing the *Scharnhorst* from escaping, and in pounding her so badly that her ability to fight back was greatly reduced. While 'Ultra' and radar

Aftermath

helped put the Royal Naval battleship in the right place at the right time, it was her firepower that was the deciding factor in the battle. During the engagement she fired at least eighty broadsides, each involving most, if not all, of her 14-inch guns. In the process she scored at least thirteen hits, using a combination of radar and visual fire control. It was an impressive performance.

Other British warships also contributed to the pounding that reduced the upper decks and superstructure of the *Scharnhorst* into a blazing shambles – the *Jamaica*, in particular, scored multiple hits with her 6-inch guns during the final phase of the battle. But gunnery alone proved incapable of sinking the *Scharnhorst*. Her armoured belt protected her lower hull, and while the ship was damaged and virtually disabled, she was still floating. The job of finishing off the German warship was undertaken by torpedoes, fired by a combination of destroyers and light cruisers at ranges of less than 2 miles. It was these torpedoes that ripped through the hull, causing the *Scharnhorst* to sink. In effect, they could reach the vitals of the ship, while the shells fired by naval guns could not.

The loss of the *Scharnhorst* was a blow from which the Kreigsmarine was unable to recover. She was the last operational warship capable of attacking the Arctic convoys. The *Tirpitz* had been damaged by midget submarines earlier that year, and in 1944 she would be damaged again by a naval air strike, before being sunk by Lancaster bombers in September 1944. All hope of helping stem the flow of military aid to the Soviet Union ended when the *Scharnhorst* was lost. With it went the last chance of the Kriegsmarine to avert disaster on the Eastern Front. Above all, Hitler lost all confidence in the surface fleet. After December 1943, apart from its hard-pressed and dwindling U-boat arm, the Kriegsmarine would be little more than passive bystanders during the death throes of Germany's Third Reich.

Index

The following index is divided into three parts: General, Allied Vessels and German Vessels. At the request of the compiler, Konter-Admiral Erich Bey and *Scharnhorst* have not been referenced, as they occur *passim*.

Index

The Battle of North Cape

Index

The Battle of North Cape